© 2020 Maudlin Pond Press, LLC

Published by:

Maudlin Pond Press, LLC

PO Box 53, Tybee Island, GA 31328, USA

Typesetting: Jody Patterson

Front and Back Cover Designs: Abbigail Rigdon Murphy

A CIP record for this book is available from the Library of Congress

Cataloging-in-Publication Data

ISBN 978-1-7356192-0-0

ISBN 978-1-7356192-1-7

Printed in the USA

Swamp Goddess

True Stories from the Okefenokee Swamp

Cathy J. Sakas

Maudlin Pond Press, LLC

Dedicated to all who have experienced
the Great Okefenokee Swamp with me,
especially Suzanna Black and
Dr. Tom Wills Cofer, and in special memory
of Jim Bitler and Dr. Bob Harris.

Table of Contents

Preface

I first became enthralled with the Great Okefenokee Swamp in 1976 when I took my first trip on the Red Trail. The Red Trail is considered one of the more difficult trails in the Swamp because of the long distances between shelters. Launching at Kingfisher Landing on the central eastern side of the Swamp, the first day takes paddlers through mostly prairie for 12 miles. The open prairie is lovely especially in the spring when the flowers are blooming but it can also be treacherous if the wind is in your face and from my own personal experience, the wind always seems to be in your face.

The shelter that night is a platform called Maul Hammock. Some of the most incredible frog choruses are heard here in the spring. It is as if you are transported back to the Jurassic Period of the Mesozioc Era. The next day is 11 miles through mostly prairie again but near the end of the day,

Yellow Trail MM2 - Mizell Prairie

the trail deepens and the flow picks up speed pushing you into the deeper waterways leading into Big Water. The shelter that night is called Big Water.

The final day on the Red Trail is what I refer to as the "magic carpet ride". The nine-mile paddle goes by way too quickly. If you paddle this part of the trail on Saturday or Sunday you likely will feel intruded upon by motor boaters coming up from Stephen Foster State Park where this trail ends. I prefer to paddle entirely on weekdays when most visitors are still working. To enjoy Minnie's Lake Run on this last day is quite like hearing Beethoven's Fifth or even Ninth for the first time; it is like your first kiss with someone you adore; it is like seeing a baby smile for the first time; it is like receiving an award you weren't expecting. It is an incredible experience that you won't ever forget. It is that mesmerizing.

This book is a series of stories, true stories, selected from the many adventures I have had in the fabulous Okefenokee Swamp. My intent is to help the reader experience the exquisite greatness and

10

small magical wonders this incredible wilderness holds for all who venture into her depths and journey into her far reaches. I realize most will never see nor experience the Swamp on their own. They will not have the desire nor equipment nor perhaps stamina to experience the Swamp. So through these stories I take you along with me, with those who have gone on my excursions.

Through their adventures and mine, you will experience the joy of seeing vast stretches of uninterrupted wilderness, of expansive prairies alive with colorful flowers and of seasonally changing foliage, of stately pines and majestic cypress, of deafening frog choruses, of primordial bellowing alligators, of the often quirky human history, of strong winds, of intense lightning storms, of gorgeous sunrises, of spectacular sunsets, of melodious trumpeting cranes, of fantastical dreams realized and not. These stories are all true.

I use the names of actual people when I have their permission to do so. One story is about past public figures. In some stories the names have been changed when I have been unable to find them to ask their permission. The adventures are in the sequence of events as I remember them.

Generously woven throughout the stories are the natural and human history of this great Swamp as I understand it and have recounted it to guests and friends beginning with my first trip into the Great Okefenokee Swamp.

I began leading trips into the Okefenokee National Wildlife Refuge with my then husband John "Crawfish" Crawford to whom I remain eternally grateful for my initial infield natural history education. To this day we remain friends.

He with his two partners Richard S. (Dick) Murlless (deceased) and Joyce Bogot Murlless (long-time friend) established Wilderness Southeast, Inc. back in 1973. The company, now referred to simply as WiSE, the first of its kind in the southeast, paved the way for other ecotourism-based businesses.

Wilderness Southeast expanded over many decades with its trip offerings ranging from backpacking trips in the Appalachian Mountains of North Carolina, to boating explorations of Georgia's estuaries and barrier islands, to canoeing and kayaking trips in the Okefenokee and Everglades, to snorkeling and sailing trips into the Florida Keys and Dry Tortugas. Eventually international trips to Central and South America and the Bahamas were added. Alas, WiSE's overnight trips became a victim of specialization. Specialist companies offering guided trips into only one ecosystem eventually outcompeted WiSE, the generalists. Presently WiSE offers day trips into local wilderness areas around Savannah and throughout Coastal Georgia.

More recently, I relish spending time with friends and therefore they are my first choice for paddling companions. I still do occasionally accept paying trips from those who really want me to lead their trips. My fees are fair but not inexpensive.

To date, I have led well over 300 trips ranging in length from one to four nights into the famous Okefenokee Swamp and I am not done yet!

So, please, sit back with a good reading light and settle in for some exciting, often humorous adventures in the comfort of your own space albeit without the heat or cold, rain, humidity, biting insects and intense weather episodes. Join me on fabulous journeys into the Great Okefenokee Swamp!

Enjoy the Paddle!

Cathy J. Sakas (aka Swamp Goddess)

2 July 2020

Orange Trail MM3 in Suwannee Canal

Introduction

The great expanse of wild beauty known as the Okefenokee Swamp tucks into the southeastern corner of Georgia and spills over into the northeastern corner of Florida. The black waters of St. Mary's River serve as the border between northeastern Florida and southeastern Georgia and is one of the few rivers in North America that flows east, south, east again, north and east once more on its journey from Swamp to Sea.

St. Mary's River drains about 15% of the Okefenokee to the east while the Suwannee River drains the lion's share of it to the west emptying into the Gulf of Mexico. As both rivers exit the southern boundary of the Okefenokee, their waters are dark, nearly black, made so by the tannins leaching from depositions of leaves, bark, twigs, limbs and trunks. The water, relatively warm year round and slow moving, steeps the plant debris into a very strong acidic black tea. The water's acidity is comparable to that of colas, citrus juices and beer.

The black water's high acidity does not allow bacteria nor fungi to thrive. Consequently, the water in the inner reaches of the Okefenokee where motor boats are not permitted, is relatively safe to drink or at least to use for cooking and clean up. I recommend however that if you intend to drink swamp water, you bring a filter. Plant debris does not entirely break down, remaining suspended in the water column. A bandana, and any cloth of similar thread density, work just fine. Too finely gauged water filters clog up requiring continuous cleaning and will therefore not yield much filtered water for drinking. Coffee or tea made from filtered swamp water is quite tasty.

The Okefenokee Swamp is approximately 20 miles wide by about 35 miles long or approximately 700 square miles or about 448,000 acres of federally protected wilderness. It is officially called the Okefenokee National Wildlife Refuge, a bureau within the U.S. Department of the Interior.

The Swamp encompasses vast shallow-water grassy plains called prairies. The dominant plant cover there is maiden cane along with sedges and reeds. In the deeper lakes, majestic cypress trees with huge buttressing trunks dominate with equally impressive buttressed gums, red maples, hollies, and bays. On the sandy islands, stately pines dominate with oaks, loblolly bays, magnolias, birches and wax myrtle. The Okefenokee however is mostly comprised of the expansive prairies punctuated with the tall straight dark green skylines of pine islands and silhouetted with feathery-needled cypress domes.

Throughout the seasons various plants bloom and diverse birds arrive with trilling melodious whistles, burrs and chirps. In the spring the prairies are especially alive, awash in color. The pinks of orchids, the violets of iris, the canary yellow of golden clubs, the alabaster whites of lilies, the yellow of yellow water bonnets are so very breathtakingly

Neverwets or Goldenclubs (*Orontium aquaticum*)

beautiful. Carnivorous plants are quite lovely too from the diminutive rose-pink flowers of the subtle sundews to the big showy yellow blossoms of the pitcher plants. Songbirds of all kinds pass through and some nest. Small male Prothonotary Warblers in particular are quite noticeable in their fine mating plumage of bright canary yellow, looking quite like small flying finger bananas.

In spring the statuesque cypress trees begin leafing out in early March with vibrant yellowish green needles that darken to a deeper forest green as the season waxes. Alligators begin stirring from their lethargic fast of the winter months when their body temperatures drop too low to allow their metabolisms to properly digest food. As air temperatures warm, their metabolisms rev up catalyzing their appetites for food and sex. In early spring these last vestiges of dinosaurs begin their 180 million-years' old mating rituals. Both males and females bellow in deep guttural primordial rumblings that roar throughout the Swamp. You feel the rumblings in your sternum, more than in your ears.

In summer, tiny blossoms of yellow eye grass burst like miniature fireworks from small flower heads at the free end of stalks that reach upwards of three feet tall. Summer, alas, is not a particularly good time to venture into the Swamp unless you do not mind sweltering heat, oppressive humidity, intense afternoon thunderstorms with earth-striking bolts, and relentless swarms of biting insects, day and night. With long distances in between shelters, it is best to take an hour or two out-and-back trip in the early morning hours when heat, humidity, lightening and bugs are less.

In fall, tickseed sunflowers dominate with bright yellow petals surrounding dark centers of tiny black seeds that

Cypress Needles Changing to Fall Colors

really do look like newly hatched ticks. Also in the fall, cypress needles turn a russet brown eventually senescing to carpet the black water's surface. Cypress are one of only two deciduous conifers in North America.

Late fall through winter and into early spring Greater Sandhill Cranes join resident Florida Sandhill Cranes feasting on frogs, snakes, crawfish and other small soft and crunchy treats. The melodious staccato duets of trumpeting pair-bonded couples echo through the trees and across the prairies. In late winter eerily beautiful green orchids emerge concentrated in certain areas. Sprinkled throughout the prairies are peat blowups, layers of accumulated peat on the swamp bottom that have literally been blown up to the surface by methane gas.

Methane is a byproduct of decomposition and since the high acidity of the black water suppresses bacteria and fungi growth, decomposition is consequently very slow. It may take years for enough methane to accumulate to blow a large chunk of peat layer up to the surface. However once the peat reaches the surface and is exposed to oxygen, the peat is so fertile that seeds born on the wind and/or deposited by birds take off.

Cover plants grow rapidly stabilizing the blowup and eventually do well enough to allow shrubs to succeed, which in turn provide enough stability to afford the growth of small trees. Young trees send out lateral roots and shallow tap roots so when walking on a peat blowup the small trees sway. The blowup works like a trampoline giving way under the weight and then springing back up as the weight moves on.

Maturing trees will eventually send roots down through the blowup to secure the tree directly to the swamp floor. When the peat blowup becomes stabilized, it is then referred to as a tree island. Tree islands typically consist of wax myrtle, bays, red maples and gums. Cypress domes develop around deeper depressions to give a gentle rolling wave-like skyline to the Swamp with taller trees in the middle where the water is deeper.

To understand the other way islands form in the Okefenokee and any other southeastern swamp, one has to go back hundreds of thousands of years when the Swamp became exposed as dry ground. Ocean water drawn up into the polar ice caps caused the sea level to recede. At the peak of Earth's last ice age, the Wisconsin Ice Age, 17,000 years ago the southeastern coastline shifted 60 miles further offshore than todays.

As ocean water receded during the Wisconsin Ice Age, what is now the Okefenokee Swamp dried out and her former swamp floor supported by ocean water began to weaken, forming small shallow depressions. Concomitantly prevailing winds coming out of the northwest pushed up sandy soil on the southeastern lip of the depressions. This explanation is the most accepted for the formation of the crescent shaped larger islands that populate the Okefenokee.

The largest island is Cowhouse Island at the northern edge of the swamp. On the southwestern side is Billy's Island which is easily accessible by motor boat or kayak or canoe from Stephen Foster State Park near Fargo. Another island easily accessible is Chesser Island. You can actually drive to that one by entering Suwannee Canal Recreation Area near Folkston.

These islands and several more are crescent shaped and populated with tall stately pines, mostly loblolly and slash. When I paddle on the canoe trails approaching Billy's Island or Floyd's Island or Mixon's Hammock, I look for a change in the treeline, specifically for the dark green bushy tops of pines. Pines only grow on islands that are relatively dry, which are the larger crescent-shaped sandy-soil islands. The sandy soil belies the Okefenokee's past as ocean habitat as late as 140,000 years ago.

For more information on the natural and human history of the Okefenokee Swamp, all one has to do is access the great worldwide web. I suggest accessing the official U.S. Department of the Interior's Okefenokee National Wildlife Refuge website as well as the New Georgia Encyclopedia.

Several books are on the market as well. Three of my favorites are:

1. Queen of the Okefenokee by Lois Barefoot Mays and Richard H. Mays. Biography of Ms. Lydia Smith, a giant of a woman physically and in business.

2. Okefinokee Album by Francis Harper. Photo-journal of naturalist, Francis Harper who visited the Swamp in the early to mid-1900's.

3. Swampwise by Okefenokee Joe. Wonderfully entertaining and educationally rich, it is also a video with Okefenokee Joe's song "Swampwise" featured.

For information about specific flora and fauna, the best free apps are PictureThis and iNaturalist. When you determine the general identification of your entity, then you can access other apps for more specific identifications and information.

I encourage you to go outside to enjoy and explore your natural world wherever you happen to be. You will feel better for it!

In the meantime, join me in Swamp Goddess: True Stories from the Okefenokee Swamp.

Enjoy the Adventures!

Cathy J. Sakas
aka Swamp Goddess
2 July 2020

Perfect Mirror Image of Trees

CHAPTER 1

Too Tall Paul

Floyd's Island

Fall 1983

Too Tall Paul grunted involuntarily as his canoe bumped ashore on Floyd's Island.

Bending forward at the waist with knees extended outside his hips, he pulled his sizable bulk forward with hands on the gunnels.

His cramped knees, in dire need of unfolding and straightening, had been in his chest all day long.

Too Tall Paul continued stretching forward, then upward. Releasing the gunnels, he rose to his full height of 6'9" while still in the canoe. An impressive sight.

Jim, his paddling partner and my co-leader, still seated in the stern, said, "Ya know, watchin' you unfurl like that is like watching a tree grow in time lapse. You really must've been ready to stand up by mile two."

Too Tall Paul, now stretching in earnest, grunted in agreement.

Pausing mid-stretch, he took off his jaunty green felt broad-brimmed hat that sported the long, alabaster-white Great Egret feather he plucked from the water earlier in the day and stuck in the brown leather hat band. And thusly revealed his perfect, unblemished shiny bald head.

A bright yellow ray of sunlight piercing through the tree branches glinted off his smooth, naturally polished scalp like a bright beacon signaling from a lighthouse.

Glowing inwardly and now outwardly, Too Tall Paul very happily stepped on to Floyd's Island's terra firma in the world famous Okefenokee Swamp with his knees where they were meant to be - below his hips and not just below eye level.

Too Tall twisting around from his waist, admired the lovely woods lining the footpath for a few seconds.

"Nice place you have here, Jimbo."

"Yeah, thanks, I rather like it myself. Now be a good fella and pull me up."

Too Tall did as requested. Taking a few short, scuffling steps backwards to pull the canoe up onto land, his left foot squished directly into a pile of crap.

"Oh gross! Yuck! What th' heck? I come all this long way to be in wilderness, and the last thing I expect to do is step right into a pile of shit!"

Instinctively, he shook his foot, trying to throw off the odorous mess. But it stuck.

Jim couldn't help but laugh, "Yep, it's a crime. No doubt a gift from the island's famed resident male bobcat Robert. Probably deposited only moments before we landed. Just step to the side of the trail and

Barred Owl Overhead in West Entrance to Floyd's Island

scrape your foot in the weeds, so no one else steps in it."

Their canoe wended first through the water-trail's serene entrance to Floyd's Island, beneath an arboreal version of a cathedral's vaulted arch. Elegant red maples with bright green, red-stemmed leaves; ashy smooth-barked, green-leaved and red-berried hollies; comically buttressed tupelos; and majestic feather-needled cypress lined the sinuous approach.

Jim spotted a Barred Owl sleepily roosting in a branch ten feet overhead. Fortunately it stayed put and afforded everyone with cameras the chance to snap a nice close up.

I had led groups down this gorgeous waterway many times before. Magnanimously, I wanted Jim and Too Tall Paul, who had been in the sweep position all day, to have that same quiet rush, that titillating thrill of leading the procession through this hallowed natural cathedral.

Until the fires of 2011 and 2012, paddling into Floyd's

Western Approach to Floyd's Island

Island from the east side had been like entering the most beautiful of sanctuaries. It stirred me more than any man-made structure of worship I had seen so far. The pure forces of nature built this cathedral. The very hands of the Great Spirit. Mother Nature. Gaia. Perfect in all ways.

One of my three favorite sections in the entire Swamp, I didn't get to see this one nearly as often as the other two, River Narrows and Minnie's Lake Run, on the southwestern side of the Okefenokee.

This section of trail evoked the most reverence in me of the three. Especially because I and therefore my group were always assured of being the only ones to experience it on any given day. Like being the only pilgrims to Shangri-La.

The refuge management schedules one group per day per trail. Therefore it is very rare to ever meet another group on your reserved trail.

Day users frequent River Narrows and Minnie's Lake Run. Mostly in noisy, smelly motor boats. Here in the eastern approach to Floyd's Island, there are never any motor boats. They are prohibited this far on the trail system.

In the many decades I have enjoyed the Swamp, only one time have I met another group. An anomaly. A departing group was forced to retrace its path to get off the island when the water was too low on the western side. Today the approach to Floyd's was magnificent, and it was too bad that Too Tall's reverie was rudely interrupted by his inauspicious step into Robert Bobcat's pile of freshly deposited crap.

"So why would a bobcat choose to do his business in the middle of the trail?" asked Too Tall.

"Well, I suspect old Robert heard us coming down the waterway as soon as we entered the approach over a mile back. He just doesn't like sharing his island with us bipeds, so I'm told," answered Jim matter-of-factly. "Cathy told me about Robert and said to be on the look-out for him. Only the first arrivals to the island ever get a glimpse of him, and he always leaves his calling card, daring any and all to cross his marked line."

"Really? Bobcats are that calculating? They dare you to cross their boundary line by marking it with their excrement?"

"Yep, really. Bobcats, and all cats for that matter, are very calculating when it comes to defending and claiming territory. They let you know it's their turf in a rather malodorous way as you just experienced.

Cabin on Floyd's Island Built in 1925 by Hebard Lumber Company

Sometimes it's firsthand; sometimes it's first foot."
Jim chuckled. Too Tall did not.

Too Tall Paul shook his head in disgust as he absorbed
this new bit of feline information. Muttering under
his breath, he did as instructed and moved the pile
of excrement off the trail. He cleaned his shoe in the
weeds, so others wouldn't be in receipt of Robert's
lovely calling card.

Canoe by canoe, the rest of our party arrived. Too Tall
and Jim helped them pull up onto land and instructed
them to carry their gear up to the campsite. We would
come back to transport the empty canoes across
the island after we set up camp. Ready for our next
morning's departure on the western trail exit.

By the time I arrived with Jeannie, my well-seasoned
bow partner, most of the work was done. There was
a little method to my madness in letting Jim and Too
Tall go first. Magnanimity indeed!

Everyone set up their tents in what they deemed the
best spots, away from the historic cabin constructed by
Hebard Lumber Company. The well-built hewn-cypress

Jim Bitler

log cabin with a roof of overlapping cypress shakes was used as a hunting lodge during their cypress timbering days from 1909 to 1927 and afterwards into the 1940's.

Jim and I warned our mostly novice campers about spreading their sleeping bags in the inviting rustic cabin. We knew the resident mice would keep them awake all night long. I never slept in the cabin myself just because I noticed mice droppings on previous trips. Those who were unwise in not heeding their leaders' instructions were indeed very sorry throughout the night and very sleepy all the next day.

We packed one four-person tent just for Too Tall Paul. We knew from his application that he was a big man. A VERY BIG MAN at 6'9" and 280 pounds.

We asked people reserving spaces on our trips these

type of personal questions for practical reasons. We really needed to know physical sizes to accommodate everyone comfortably. Too Tall Paul was definitely outside the normal range. Our standard-issue two-person tent would have simply been too small for Too Tall. So we packed the four-person tent just for him and didn't assign him a tent partner. Even with him occupying the tent alone, we knew he would be cramped.

After setting up camp, we portaged our many canoes from the east side of Floyd's to the western side, whence we would depart in the morning. Four or six of us hefted each canoe to spread out the weight, and in short order we accomplished the task made quick and easy with many hands.

I offered to lead a short walk around the island for those who still had energy. Everyone did. So we set off to the west towards the mound and cypress stand.

I began by giving them a brief human history of Floyd's Island.

"Floyd's Island is named for General Charles Rinaldo Floyd who was sent into the Okefenokee to hunt down and eradicate the Seminole Indians. The Seminole had migrated into the Swamp from middle Florida as white settlers encroached on their home territory and hunting grounds. The Okefenokee was their last refuge. The story goes that General Floyd and his men entered the inhospitable, terrifying Swamp with great trepidation, only to engage a very small band of Seminoles. They killed one and wounded another. Their leader, most likely Billy Bowlegs, had led the bulk of his band back into Florida to rejoin other Seminoles, and that apparently worked."

I wove a personal anecdote into my running narrative.

"Years ago my husband Chris introduced me to his friend named Maxie Wildes, who was originally from

29

the Waycross area. It took a few minutes for his name to light up my memory chips, but they finally made the association."

"I asked, 'Your name is the same as a family of Wildes I read about who were massacred by Seminole Indians in the late 1830's around the Okefenokee Swamp. Seems the Indians took issue with settlers' land and game infringements. Are you related in some way to that family?'"

"You can imagine my great surprise when Maxie said, 'Why yes, I am! My great, great, great grandfather was a member of that unfortunate family living near Waresboro at that time. He was the youngest and the smallest. On that fateful day of July 22nd, 1838, he was the only one to escape. He was so small that the Seminoles overlooked him as he hid under the bed. When no one was looking, he escaped through an open window. The story goes that he just kept running until he couldn't run anymore. Fortunately another settler family found him huddled up against a tree and took him in and raised him. I am a result of his will to survive and his adoptive family's

Logging Skidder

benevolence.'"

"'And so you're named for him?'"

"'Well, he was such an extraordinary character in our family that many males bear his name. I am Maxie Wildes IV.'"

"Wow! I was meeting a living piece of history."

I continued weaving my side story. "I found this to be ironic since my husband Chris, Maxie's experimental aircraft flying buddy, is part Blackfoot Indian. Time is the great healer of all wounds, ya know. Perhaps generations ago these two would have been zinging arrows or bullets at each other. Now they're big men playing with their very big and way too expensive toys, albeit peacefully now."

Everyone chuckled. They truly appreciated the story as much as I did telling it.

We walked over to the high mound off to the southwest side of the cabin, and I picked up the original story line again.

"This mound was cut through to accommodate the tramway that moved timbered cypress from Floyd's to Billy's Island and from Billy's to Waycross where the main saw mills were located. During the heyday of Hebard Lumber Company's cypress logging no one was particularly interested in nor sensitive to the Indian cultures. But it was a big surprise when the men digging into this mound for construction engineering reasons hit these Timucua skeletons. And they were amazed that, when the skeletons were pieced together, some of the males stretched into frames that were seven feet tall!"

As is human nature, everyone instinctively turned their eyes toward Too Tall Paul. We are really quite funny, we humans.

Virginia Whitetail Deer with Swampman Muss on Floyd's Island Dec. 2018
(Photo by Steve Farace, Sweetwater Brewing)

Too Tall looked around, surprised, "Ah, don't look at me, folks. I got my height I'm sure from all the hormones in the cow's milk I was fed in my baby bottle. And besides, I'm actually a descendent of the Spaniards, and they're not tall at all, or at least they weren't back then."

That bit of information sparked my very overactive imagination.

"I can only imagine what it must have been like for those Spaniards in Hernando de Soto's exploration party of the 1540's. They were the first Europeans to encounter the Calusa in south Florida and then the Timucua up here. Records indicate the Spaniards at that time were short people. The men were maybe five feet tall or so. So, I can just hear the conversation. '*Mierda, Hernando, estos nativos son gigantes!*' Some of the Calusa males were seven-footers as well."

"Eventually these skeletons made their way to archaeologists who determined they were of the Weeden Island culture, burial mound builders. The skeletons were well over 1000 years old. The big chief and his entourage were buried in these mounds. Artifacts - shell bead necklaces, shell ear pins, earlobe plugs of fish swim bladders, pottery

- are typically found alongside the heavily tattooed bodies."

I was on a roll with the rapt attention of my group, so I pressed on with more information.

"Lithographs surviving from that period clearly show the Calusa and Timucua with full-body tattoos. Males and females began accumulating tattoos as they aged and took on increasing responsibilities. The heaviest tattooing clearly identified the head male. The men also wore their hair pulled up into top knots on top of their heads, which added a few more inches to their already towering presence."

Again, everyone instinctively looked at Too Tall. He was now our working model of a Timucua. The only problem was the lack of hair on top of his shiny bald head that could be gathered into a top knot. No tattoos showing either. But we could fix the latter.

"When I worked for NOAA, I had the good fortune to spend over a week in American Samoa with colleagues there. The husband of my counterpart in Pago Pago had a full body tattoo. Of course I asked how the tattooing was accomplished, and he gave me a blow-by-blow, literally, detailed account of the traditional method. And it is brutal. The method used on him I am sure was similar to the method used by the Calusa and Timucua. My friend's husband however had the benefit of strong alcohol to get him through the nine days, five hours per day, of the very painful ordeal."

"The skin is broken by pounding sharpened bones into it. Once the pattern is made in the skin, ashes moistened with saliva are pressed into the wound to darken it. When healed, the tattoo appears a very dark gray against russet brown skin. It is quite beautiful artistically."

"My American Samoan friend is boldly, beautifully

Great Blue Heron Taking Flight

tattooed from mid-calf all the way up to mid-torso as
is his culture's tradition. He reported the hardest area
was his stomach. He had to tense his abdominal muscles
to make a stiff enough platform for the bones to be
pounded into his skin to break it. Ouch." I grimaced,
still empathetic to his description. So did everyone
else.

"In lithographs, the male Timucua are tattooed from
their ankles all the way up the back of their plucked
heads. The tattoos are in fine parallel lines that curve
and weave around the body. Same in Calusa lithographs.
The tattoos were not of animals, sweethearts' nor moms'
faces, crosses, skulls, anchors, motorcycles, words, etc.
like we see today."

Good natured conversation ensued about whether Too
Tall wanted us to tattoo him in the traditional manner.
He emphatically declined. Pointing out that: (a.) he
had not seen any suitable bones for sharpening to do a
proper job; and (b.) there wasn't nearly enough alcohol

34

on hand for sterilizing purposes and for numbing pain.

Two good points.

I could have found a bone or an antler though. We did have plenty of rubbing alcohol on hand for the sterilization part. However, I am quite sure there would have been a mutiny if all the available drinkable alcohol had been spent numbing Too Tall senseless for the bone-pounding part.

While we continued our exploration of the area, still ribbing Too Tall about tattooing him, Jeannie suddenly asked, "Are there coral snakes in the Swamp?"

"Yep, they are here but I've only seen one so far, and that was at the boardwalk on Chesser Island where, ironically enough, there is lots of tourist traffic. What brought that up?" I asked.

"Well, I think I just saw one go in that hole in the log over there," she said as she pointed in the direction of a rather large green moss-carpeted horizontal log.

"Okay, let's have a look!"

We all moved in the direction Jeannie pointed. To my great surprise, and delight actually, a rather large coral snake holed up in a hollow of that nurse log. Elegantly slender, its bright vivid bands of yellow, red, and black indicated it must have just molted. I guessed it approached, but still shy of, its maximum length of four feet. It was stunningly gorgeous!

Coral snakes are noted for being docile. It really takes a lot to rile one up to striking level. Over my many years out in the wilds, I have learned not to be a "snatch and grab" naturalist, preferring instead to observe an animal doing its natural thing in its natural habitat without the stress of being grabbed.

I learned my lesson a long time ago when I was a

young gung-ho "snatch and grab" naturalist with a group of first graders. I saw a very slender, beautiful, shiny black racer gracefully draped in a wax myrtle branch. I knew she would move before all of the kids could see her, so I snatched her up.

Only problem was, she moved just as my hand neared her neck. My snatch landed too far down her slender body. This gave the very frightened, and now in hyper self-defense mode, black racer enough neck length to firmly plant her mouth onto the highly vascularized fleshy area of my hand.

And then she struck six more times before I could get her under control.

Her razor-sharp teeth cut into the soft skin between my thumb and index finger. Blood poured out of her mouth, flowing off my hand. The kids were horrified. So was I. For the kids. Not for me. Not good though.

Thenceforth I became a reformed "snatch and grab" naturalist and much more respectful of the subjects of my observations.

So we were content to observe the lovely coral snake's contrasting red and yellow bands. Her black bands blended into the dark hollow of the log.

The phrase for remembering the difference between the near-look-alike non-venomous scarlet king snake and a venomous coral snake is this:

Red on black, friend of Jack (non-venomous scarlet kingsnake). Red on yellow, kill a fellow (venomous coral snake).

It's a good phrase to remember if you frequent Sandhill environments of the southeastern USA.

Coral snakes are known for being very docile. Several anecdotes on record report coral snake bites mostly

Canebrake Rattlesnake on Billy's Island

involving children who have played with the pretty little snakes all day long. When the snake has finally had enough, it bites.

Venom of a coral snake is neurotoxic, like that of a cobra and Cleopatra's famous Egyptian asp.

In comparison, the venom of most of our venomous snakes in the Southeast – diamondback rattlers, pygmy rattlers, copperheads, water moccasins (or cottonmouths), and canebrakes (or timber rattlers) – is hemotoxic.

The difference is that hemotoxins destroy tissue while neurotoxins paralyze the nervous system.

If you survive a neurotoxic bite, there is little evidence

you were bitten.

Hemotoxic bites are a different story. Those bites can have big, visible impacts depending on how much toxin is delivered in the bite. People bitten by very agitated large eastern diamondback rattlesnakes delivering a full dose of venom in one bite have lost limbs and in some cases their lives.

Because they can attain such a large size, eastern diamondback rattlesnakes are considered among the top ten deadliest snakes in the world. Right up there with mambas, boomslangs, and fer-de-lances.

Venomous snakes can control how much venom is released per bite. If a large diamondback rattler delivers a full load in one bite, it can be deadly, especially for recipients already in a compromised state of health.

Our very lovely, docile coral snake let us move her about with a stick so we could snap good pictures. She was most accommodating and didn't try to bite once.

Another interesting fact about coral snakes is that their teeth are fixed and short. They are rarely capable

Broad Headed Skink on Floyd's Island Cabin

of even biting through socks.

We completed our walkabout and returned to camp to cook dinner. And to savor the highly appreciated end-of-the-day wine poured into out-stretched Sierra cups. The day's observations were discussed. Amiable laughs of just plain good camaraderie rang out around the lovely, happily crackling campfire.

One of the nice advantages of being on Floyd's Island is that you can actually light a fire. Fires on wooden platforms are officially forbidden, but all of them bear fire scars. Some campers just have to have a fire and think they can manage one on a wooden platform. I've always wondered what they would do if one got out of control. They certainly would be out of luck for the night!

After the last drop of this night's wine ration dripped from the last bottle and the last marshmallow roasted and the last chuckle chuckled, Jim, the last person at the fire, spread the coals and moved the unburned wood away from the ring.

Gator Buddies at Floyd's Island East Approach

39

We were safe and secure for the night.

By the time I reached my tent, muffled snoring already emanated from some of the tents. Men sleeping in the distance. Years of leading these trips taught me to pitch my tent away from everyone else, especially big men. Snoring and snorting from gents other than my own dear husband did not make for pleasant sleep.

Before dropping off, I listened to Barred Owls pair bonding with their monkey-like calls. I heard raccoons snapping twigs as they foraged around the campfire for scraps of food that had accidentally escaped our plates. I even heard the very high pitched "seep, seep, seep" of southern flying squirrels. In my mind I could see their flat rudder-like tails and their very large, deep-black pools for eyes. Attributes well suited for their night time activities.

Eventually I drifted off.

I dreamed about dolphins for some reason. Perhaps someone had asked a question about dolphins during the day, and my brain still processed the conversation. I heard a dolphin squealing. An odd squeal to be sure. I didn't recall ever hearing that type of squeal come from a dolphin before. The squealing was unearthly.

"Cathy, Cathy, Cathy!" Jim yelled at me. "Get up! Get up! Someone's in trouble!"

As a seasoned leader, it only took a few words for me to leap to action. I unzipped my bag in an instant, my heart raced; I fumbled for my boots.

Tearing out of my tent, I raced after Jim's bouncing flashlight trail. He trotted towards the source of the screams.

I knew they were not coming from my dolphin. Huh, no dolphins in the Swamp? Who knew?

We reached the largest tent in the camp. Too Tall Paul still caterwauled.

A man's scream is quite unnerving. It is not like a woman's practiced scream. We know how to scream instinctively from birth. Men, on the other hand, do not scream well. It is a most unpleasant, blood-curdling sound when one does.

Too Tall sat upright in his tent.

Jim shined his light downward and around so as not to blind Too Tall. A dim wash of light showed Too Tall's panicked face.

"Hey there, big guy, what's going on?" Jim calmly tried to ascertain the problem.

"Uh, uh, uh!" is all Too Tall could manage. His big heart raced, and his big chest heaved.

"Calm down there, big fella," Jim continued. "Can you tell us what happened? Did you have a bad dream, or are you hurt?"

"Head, head hurt," Too Tall panted, pointing to the top of his head.

Jim raised his flashlight around the side of Too Tall up to his bald head to illuminate it. There on the top were thin red streaks. Scratches.

"Okay, just a few scratches, nothing big. Nothing catastrophic. Cathy, please go get the first aid kit," Jim said as calmly as he could, so he wouldn't add to Too Tall's already heightened state of alarm.

I backed away from Too Tall's sight, slowly, calmly. Then I ran, stumbling along the way, back to my tent. I hadn't thought to grab my flashlight when Jim first woke me up, so navigating the path back to my tent in the dark required concentration to not trip and fall.

The light sleepers in our little group called out to me as I ran past their tents. I yelled back to wait a few minutes.

I found my tent. Felt around the tent floor for the cold metal of my flashlight. Found it. Shined the light. Grabbed the first aid kit.

Racing back to the scene of the crime, I processed what I had seen. I just couldn't imagine how in the world Too Tall Paul had managed to get those wounds on his lovely, unblemished, shiny head in the middle of the night.

Perhaps he was a sleep walker and had run into a branch. Maybe he had left food in his tent, and a raccoon scratched through the tent, and his head was in the way.

I just wasn't sure about this one.

After we patched Too Tall up, we promised we would determine what happened and report in the morning if everyone would get back to their tents.

With all that screaming, we couldn't just pass it off to the Barred Owls.

Great Horned Owl

42

Those who had been awakened would be curious. The hard-core sound sleepers would be too, when they heard the conversations the next morning. At least the onlookers were moving back to their tents now.

Still sitting upright, Too Tall's breathing had returned pretty much back to normal. Rattled but okay, we assured him we would get to the bottom of his midnight mystery.

Like two crime scene investigators, Jim and I set about with flashlights in hand to figure out just what had happened. We asked Too Tall a lot of questions while the incident was still fresh in his mind and on his head.

In the morning we reported our findings as if presenting evidence in a court trial.

Empirical evidence:

1. Narrow red scratches, evenly spaced, on top of Too Tall Paul's previously unblemished and untattooed bald head.

2. Shredded tent wall at the bulge where Too Tall's head pressed against it.

Bobcat Droppings (not Robert Bobcat's)

3. Agouti patterned fur on the outside tent wall.

Conclusions:

1. Too Tall Paul was so tall that, when he stretched his full length to sleep, his head pressed against the tent wall in one corner and his feet against the opposite diagonal corner.

2. Approximately 40% of body heat is lost through the head. The many tiny blood vessels in the scalp allow for heat exchange.

3. Too Tall generated so much heat out of the top of his head that he warmed up the tent wall and surrounding air to a nice, toasty level.

4. An animal, most likely Robert the resident bobcat, zeroed in on the newfound source of warmth and lay against Too Tall's head on the outside of the tent.

5. In the middle of the night Too Tall became too hot because Robert Bobcat provided an unexpected and unwanted layer of insulation to his head.

6. Too Tall reached up to remove the unwanted insulation from his very hot head.

7. Too Tall's hand hit Robert on the rump, which launched the nimble bobcat into quick departure, with claws digging into Too Tall's bald head for traction.

8. Too Tall was rudely awakened by Robert's startled escape as he left another signature feline calling card etched on to the top of Too Tall Paul's head.

9. Too Tall Paul's screams awoke all but the heaviest sleepers and no doubt gave Robert an anxiety attack.

Epilog:

This was the first and only time I have ever had an encounter like this in the Swamp. You just can't make this stuff up!

In all the many, many times I have led trips through the Swamp, I can count encounters in this bizarre category on one hand.

To my knowledge Too Tall Paul did not report any ill effects from Robert's sudden departure off his head.

Someone in the group suggested we rub ashes into the fresh scars scratched on to Too Tall Paul's head. Too Tall declined the offer stating that he didn't want to have a permanent reminder of this event as a native-rendered tattoo on his head.

To my knowledge Too Tall Paul did not return to explore the Swamp by canoe nor kayak. He reasoned a motor boat or small barge would be a better fit.

Happily, I saw Robert Bobcat and his famous calling cards for several more years.

I dutifully sent a photo to Too Tall's last known address of Robert's calling card snapped on subsequent trips to Floyd's Island until the last letter returned as undeliverable.

Regrettably, I never heard from Too Tall Paul again, but I will never forget him.

Canoes on Billy's Lake

CHAPTER 2

Land of Trembling Earth

Round Top

Spring 1989

"Land of Trembling Earth" is the English interpretation of the Creek Indian word for the great swamp located in the southeastern corner of Georgia, the world-famous Okefenokee Swamp.

The Creek people spread across coastal Georgia and north central Florida, until, under Andrew Jackson's Indian Removal Act, they were marched westward on the infamous and brutal Trail of Tears. But the lyrical names they gave to the many rivers of the region endure to this day. Ogeechee, Oconee, Ohoopee, Ocmulgee, Withlacoochee, Suwannee, Ohklocknee, etc. Look at a map of the two states, and you will discover many more. And look up the etymology of the euphonious words too. Creek words ending in "ee" denote water.

"Okefenokee" or "land of trembling earth" describes a real physical phenomenon. Submerged peat is literally blown to the surface from below when methane, a byproduct of decomposition, builds up beneath it. Peat itself is compacted layered plant debris that accumulates on the swamp bottom.

Millennia of plant debris deposition results in very acidic water from the high concentrations of tannin leached out from that plant debris. I have measured the pH (relative acidity) in some places to be as low as 3.7. By comparison, the pH of distilled vinegar is 2.4.

The pH scale ranges from 0 to 14 with 0 the most acidic and 14 the most basic. Rain water and tap water are considered neutral at close to a pH of 7.0. The pH scale is exponential; so a pH of 6.0 is ten times more acidic than 7.0, while 5.0 is a hundred times more acidic than 7.0, and 4.0 a thousand times more acidic than 7.0. You get the picture. The Swamp is very acidic!

While some bacteria and fungi are present, it is a tough environment. They are not abundant, and those that are able to survive in the very acidic water only slowly chug along, decomposing at a snail's pace. This very slow decomposition rate is the reason the peat builds up so deeply.

You might say that in the South we make tea every day, at home and in our waterways. Our rivers and swamps are referred to as black water, and they actually do appear black when looking down on to the surface. However, if you scoop up some in a clear glass and hold it to the light, you will see that it is actually a very dark, reddish-brown tea color.

In the coastal plains of Georgia, temperatures are relatively warm year round. And, because there is little change in elevation throughout the coastal plains, our water is slow-moving. These are the very conditions perfect for brewing tea.

Over time peat piles up into layers many feet thick.

Gator on Peat Blowup

In the great Okefenokee Swamp it can be 60 to 100 feet thick in some places.

As you paddle along the trails, especially in the shallow prairies, every now and then you will see small blowups bubble to the surface. On very rare occasions you may see a large blowup surface. I once saw such a big one, probably 100 square feet, rise before my eyes. Like time-lapse creation footage, let me tell you, it was impressive. At first I thought the fabled "Okefenokee Swampy", a creature of folklore rarely spoken of today, had finally shown herself.

On trips I lead, I always ask if anyone would like to "walk" on a peat blowup. Typically there are a few takers, and it is always a fun experience. I select a particularly stable peat blowup, so that no one punches through or sinks it. On one occasion however the entire group wanted to walk on it and that took some thoughtful choreography.

I invited all the ladies out first. When they all had carefully picked their way to the center of the blowup, I asked half to jump up and down while the rest stood still. Spontaneous laughter erupted from my adventurous blowup walking women who quickly transformed into giggly little girls, delighting in the sensation of jumping and balancing on such a springy trampoline.

Next it would be the men's turn. But before the ladies could get back to their canoes as instructed, the men, itching to share in the fun, piled out of their seats on to the blowup. Not good. The added weight of the male contingent began sinking the entire little island. Mayhem ensued as did lots of excited, nervous laughter.

Some ladies made it back to their canoes with only getting wet up to their knees. Others, not as quick and nimble, landed seat-first onto the blowup, by then waist deep in water. I guffawed so hard that I nearly lost control of the situation.

Eventually I managed to bark out enough commands that we all made it back to our canoes, all wet, but buoyed by the serotonin coursing through our bodies

My Lightweight Cousin Meagan Denham Mills on Peat Blowup

from such a good long belly laugh. For peat's sake.

As trip leader, I rarely if ever ask people what they do for a living. I figure that they come on these trips to get away from their routines back home. But bits and pieces of their life stories, snippets they volunteer to share, are often revealed through the course of a trip.

At the beginning of each trip I regularly use a tried and true ice breaker as a way to introduce ourselves. The Name Game allows complete strangers to give others an insight into respective personalities or at least how you want to be viewed on a particular trip.

I have been Cathy Cormorant or even Cathy Caterpillar depending on my mood.

Cormorant because I like to fly, climb trees, and dive under water as a cormorant does. Caterpillar sometimes because of the life-changing metamorphosis one undergoes.

At any rate, in this light-hearted activity, you state, if you so choose, why you associate with a particular animal or plant. Sometimes if folks in a group already know each other, I ask the person sitting on the left to give the person to their right a name and explain why.

In this group we self-named. My co-leader, Jim Jumping Cactus. Mid-50's married couple, Richard Raccoon and Rhonda Rabbit. Friends 40-something, Connie Cougar and her 20-something companion, Carl Camel. Another mid-50's married couple, Brenda Bladderwort and Bruce Bear. Friends in their mid 30's, Ali Alligator and Tom Turtle. Single late 60's, Oscar Otter. Single mid 70's, Paul Pine. And 25-year-old, Kelly Kingfisher.

On this particular trip we were heading out to Round Top for the first night, to Floyd's Island for the second night, and then back to our launch site at Suwannee Canal Recreation Area. The weather was predicted to

Fragrant White Water Lilies

be just perfect.

It was spring, and the flowers were gloriously brilliant. Sweet aromas wafted off fragrant white water lilies in full blossom. Blue flag irises stood tall and stately in a splendid display of various shades from deep purple to lighter lavender. Golden clubs or never wets sprouted eye-catching flower spikes with golden tips and contrasting white and rose bands below.

Highly competitive male canary-yellow Prothonotary Warblers chirped and flitted across our canoes as they dive bombed any spots of yellow on clothing or equipment. Fiercely territorial characters, those male Prothonotaries.

We enjoyed a lazy, easy paddle along the nine miles of the Suwannee Canal, and then really dawdled the last three miles through Grand Prairie out to Round Top. It was a glorious day.

A pair of Florida Sandhill Cranes greeted us as we reached Round Top and stayed near the platform in spite of our activity. We tried to be quiet so as not to disturb them, but as we picked up momentum setting up camp, our noise crescendoed. The food supply nearby must have been really abundant, since that handsome leggy pair, the largest of our local birds, didn't bother to go elsewhere.

Florida Sandhill Cranes mate for life building upon repeated successes of rearing chicks. Their nests are mats of reeds and grasses piled up in the prairie grass. The altricial chicks grow quickly relying on their parents to get them through their chick stage and prepare them for fending for themselves. Birds such as quail and killdeer are precocial, ready to run and fend for themselves as soon as they hatch. Larger roosting birds such as vultures, hawks, eagles, owls, herons, egrets, and cranes are described as altricial; their chicks require many weeks and, in some cases, months of parenting to get them up to speed for surviving on their own.

We busied ourselves setting up tents and the kitchen area while trying to give one another space. This is very tricky since the platforms are not very big. Tents are

Florida Sandhill Cranes Taking Flight

essential due to the presence of mosquitoes most of the year. One time I passed on pitching a tent in the dead of mosquito-free winter, but I regretted that decision as I shivered the night away. A good tent will hold in a lot of your body heat on a cold winter's night.

We had eight tents to pitch, really a job for an engineer to figure out the placement of that many tents and still have room to cook and sit outside of our tents, but we managed in short order. Jim and I pitched our tent last so as not to take up precious space. Trip leaders always take the least desirable spot, which is usually not underneath the shelter of the platform's roof. The Swamp has its own micro-climate, so even though not predicted to rain, it can. And even if it doesn't rain, it is such a hydric (wet, high humidity) ecosystem the morning dew can be so heavy you will think it did.

To conserve space we requested that folks double up as much as possible. My co-leader and I did so. The two married couples and the friends who had signed up together were fine with sharing a tent. The three singles were not.

While pitching tents Ali Alligator asked Connie Cougar, "How do you and Carl know each other?"

Carl Camel spoke up, "Connie's daughter is my girlfriend, but she doesn't enjoy canoeing or tent camping. Connie does, so we decided this would be a nice opportunity for us to get to know each other better."

In polite small talk, Carl Camel returned, "How did you and Tom meet?"

"Oh, you know, one of those proverbial office romances. We worked together well, and now we play together really well." Ali Alligator winked, and she and Carl Camel shared

Purple Trail West of Round Top in Chase Praire

a knowing smile.

No one raised an eyebrow. Sounded good to us. The Swamp's siren song draws in any and all who will only heed her call.

That night the amorous male frogs were in fine voice. Tiny cricket frogs clicked all night long in a loud "tck, tck, tck, tck," much like steel balls tapping against each other. Carpenter frogs punctuated the night with loud staccato calls sounding like a hammer repeatedly striking a nail. Sometimes they changed it up with their ratchet-sounding calls "kachunk, kachunk, kachunk." The "rrrrrrrrrrpp, rrrrrrrrrrpp" coming from the southern leopard frog contingent sounded as if their balloon-like throats were rubbing against each other's. Froggy love, or what scientists call amplexus, was definitely in the air and would occur as soon as a choosy amphibious lady selected her horny beau.

At some point during the night a bull gator bellowed,

and that initiated a series of bellowing for quite a radius around the platform. You really don't realize how many alligators there are in any one place until they begin to bellow.

The bellows of a male or bull gator sound rather like an African lion's deep roars. I can imitate the high-pitched yelps of hatchlings but not the very deep bass bellows of the bulls. Females bellow too, but theirs are of shorter duration and are a bit higher, more in the range of a low baritone. I can manage that one sometimes on a morning when I am particularly hoarse.

No question though, the deepest and most impressive bellows go to the bulls. Water literally dances off their backs as the subsonic vibrations originating deep within their cores, cause their bodies to vibrate. The only visible sign is the dancing water on their backs that looks like heavy raindrops bouncing up after hitting the water's surface.

I was really ready for my sleeping bag when all of our evening activities were completed. We had recapped the day's activities by making a list of all the creatures seen and heard and talked about their natural history and how they all fit together to form the intricate ecosystem of this great wilderness. We discussed our agenda for the next day and said goodnight in a good-natured way.

"Good night, Papa Jim Jumping Cactus and Mama Cathy Cormorant," Ali Alligator sweetly called out.

"Nighty, night my little kings and queens of our swampy realm," Papa Jim Jumping Cactus rejoined.

It was a very amicable group, and we truly enjoyed the new friendships being made and stronger bonds forging between existing couples.

As usual I had been paired with one of the least experienced paddlers in the group. Even though there

Todd Mussman Steps Out on Peat Blowup to Become Swampman Muss

had been no wind to speak of, I was tired from being the workhorse of our canoe, my bow partner Oscar Otter more or less dead weight.

Even though you may be bone tired and typically drop off to sleep quickly, lying on a platform for the first time suspended between pilings driven deeply into spongy peat is a very different sensation. You literally feel every little movement.

Someone turning over in their sleeping bag can abruptly or gently sway the entire platform, depending on how quickly or slowly they move and on how big or small they are. I remind everyone that Okefenokee means "land of trembling earth", so they won't be surprised when they first experience the trampoline or water bed phenomenon. And so it was.

It took some who were not used to sleeping flat on the wooden planks a while to settle down. I could hear murmurs of soft conversations taking place in most of the tents. Giggles erupted here and there as they accustomed to the jiggling platform. Small playful spats erupted as imaginary territorial lines were drawn in the small tents and then breached.

Soon, convinced all my charges would survive the night, I willingly succumbed to the gentle embrace of Morpheus. Even the loud chorus of "kachunks, kachunks, rrrrrrrpps, rrrrrrrpps, and tcks, tcks, tcks" of the thousands of male frogs hoping to mate this night did not deter my sleep.

Barely an hour after I drifted off, the platform began to shake gently, but pleasantly, rhythmically. The shaking continued gently for a while and then intensified. When it became wildly urgent, I sat up fully awake, and Jim did too. We looked at each other, "Earthquake?"

Then we heard the muffled but unmistakable moans and groans of the human version of amphibian amplexus,

Camping on Round Top

Homo sapien coitus.

"Not an earthquake!"

Apparently the froggy chorus of love had inspired two in our group.

The shaking continued and grew in intensity. You could feel every urgent thrust. I really feared the posts holding up the platform, although driven deep into the peat, would not take much more of this violent movement. Our very lives were at stake, for peat's sake!

You can survive in the Swamp without a platform by pulling canoes abreast to create a makeshift platform of sorts. Outward Bound does this in the Everglades, but they prepare ahead of time. They stow long slender pliable boards in the bottoms of their canoes and at night lay them across the canoes' gunnels to form a surprisingly stable platform. We were not prepared to do that and certainly couldn't pull it off in the middle of the night anyway. My mind raced.

My ears focused in on the grunts and moans coming

Misty Morning Sunrise at Round Top

from one of the tents. One of our married couples had succumbed to the amorous siren call of our Swamp.

We now knew the reason for the quaking but not the specific couple.

As everyone else awakened to the situation too, confused questions were audible "what the...?" Then giggles began at one end of the platform and rippled across our little tent town. Our amorous duo oblivious of their audience.

To save the group and our platform, I finally spoke up like a camp counselor. "There is only a millimeter or two of cloth in these tent walls, and they do not provide the privacy you think they do. We can feel your every movement, and I do mean eeeevvvveeeeerrrryyyy movement, so stop it!"

The entire group giggled and tittered like middle schoolers, not politely, really incredulous that the amorous duo didn't have a clue they had been outed.

Eventually the romantic pair got it, and I heard the young man's and then the older woman's voices coming to realization. Connie Cougar and her daughter's boyfriend Carl Camel? Really? Yikes!

"An opportunity to get to know each other better" was how I think he put it.

Indeed! Oh My! Jim and I shook our heads and scrunched our noses. This was certainly a first. I already imagined the conversation around the dinner table when Connie Cougar and Carl Camel re-capped their trip to her daughter, his girlfriend, about getting to know each other and the frogs better.

Without any further admonition from me but a lot of murmuring from the other tents, we all eventually settled back down and drifted off to sleep again. The Cougar and her Camel audibly silent.

60

The next morning we all knew who the movers and shakers had been, and it was an interesting study to see how each person engaged the Cougar and her Camel.

Carl's name would hence forth be known as Carl Humpty Camel in conversations after the trip. Connie's moniker turned out to be prophetically spot on.

What I wanted to say was, "Good for you, Miss Cougar, cause, damn, he's a hunk but damn, he's your daughter's boyfriend." But I didn't.

Instead I politely said, "Did ya'll hear all those frogs last night? Didn't that incredibly loud chorus take you on a time travel trip back to the Jurassic?"

We all made polite small talk, but every now and again I caught eyes surreptitiously sizing up Humpty and his Cougar. I guess the women wanted to know what she had to bed such a handsome young buck and I guess the men did too. We all really struggled to keep straight faces considering we had shared the nocturnal trembling earth of love.

Just about when I thought we had all moved on, Bruce Bear, yawned while stretching his arms over his head and boldly said with an impish twinkle in his eyes, "That was the best sleep I've ever had. It felt like I was being rocked in a cradle all night long."

Brenda Bladderwort, his wife, punched him in his ample middle with her elbow.

Mouthfuls of coffee spewed in fine mists; forks tinkled on to tin plates to free a hand to stem outbursts of laughter; my Swampers spun on their heels and doubled over. All of us nearly fell off the platform in uncontrollable laughter. Connie Cougar and Carl Humpty Camel ghosted into their tiny tent of love.

Vultures

The ice had inexorably been broken. We had all
experienced the "Land of Trembling Earth" in a
completely new way.

CHAPTER 3

Ashes to Ashes

Owl's Roost Tower
Suwannee Canal Recreation Area

April 2007

Brenda sped home late April 18th after filing all of her clients' tax returns and tidying up her desk and office. After screeching into her driveway like a stunt driver, she slammed shut the door of her aging Volvo station wagon and raced up the open wooden-slat stairs into her modest stilted home on Pine Island on Florida's west coast, not far from Naples and her favorite and frequent paddling mecca, the Everglades. Already packed, she only needed to grab the last few essentials.

As she ran out the door she snatched up her keys from the large heart cockle shell on the small table by the front door. With the realization of her long-held dream of paddling the Okefenokee drawing ever so near, she threw her day pack into the passenger seat and tore back out her driveway to head north with her old faithful, now fading aquamarine, sea kayak in its permanent position locked securely in the Yakama racks on top. Brenda set herself on automatic pilot to drive through the night to reach Folkston by noon. Her thermos filled to the gills with black coffee. The first Pink Floyd tape already loaded into the player and other Pink Floyd tapes along with those of Fleetwood Mac and Journey were ready to roll. Brenda's long night's journey had begun.

On April 17th after filing her taxes through her local long-time family friend and CPA, Suzanna left Cambridge arriving in Savannah late afternoon from Logan Airport with her stuffed day pack and her "mother of a duffle" crammed to bursting with clothes, gear, paddling jacket, tent, sleeping bag, extra thick Thermarest, and small packable gifts for me and my family, who had made this Yankee an honorary member of our Savannah family. That evening we had a lovely time catching up. Suzanna brought Chris a brightly flowered extra-large Hawai'ian shirt and me an extra-large block of indescribably delicious dark chocolate. Suzanna had even knitted a small adorable mouse for Coral our orange streaked tabby filled with irresistible catnip grown in her garden. How thoughtful!

The next day, midmorning, we departed the Treehouse for Savannah International Airport in plenty of time to pick up Suzanna's newfound friend Beth.

We spotted Beth as she deplaned. Tall, blond, squeaky clean good looks, no makeup whatsoever, with the gait of a linebacker, she aptly fit Suzanna's description of corn-fed farm-raised all American Irish Catholic girl. Since Beth's flight arrived mid-morning from Indiana, we had ample time to collect her and her tightly but neatly packed bags to drive south to Folkston for a noon rendezvous with Brenda at the Okefenokee Restaurant for lunch.

I knew Suzanna well after paddling together for

Me and Suzanna

many years in the Okefenokee. Getting to know each other initially as one of many participants on trips I led, we bonded and had become good friends over the many spring and mostly fall Swamp paddling trips.

I knew Brenda too, from many kayaking forays into the Everglades. I first met her while visiting our mutual friend Mike Ward, the sociable hermit who lived on Camp Lulu Key and Float Key. Mike claimed those keys through squatter's rights, although the owners of record, the Collier family of publishing fame, begged to differ. But that is another set of stories waiting to be written.

Statuesque Brenda, amiable, dark curls tinged with gray streaks touching her wide strong shoulders, preferred to paddle kayak. I did too. On this rare occasion I would paddle solo in the Swamp, in my old faithful baby-blue Arluk III sea kayak. Brenda's preferred personal paddling style was a sprint. It would be fun pacing her, but I would have to be mindful not to lose sight of Beth and Suzanna who would be together in my slower tandem red Indian River canoe.

Suzanna, petit, five feet one inch (maybe two inches

if standing on tippy toes), silver coils springing out all over her head, very fit with the self-confidence of a disciplined woman who had lived a lot of life, had learned to accept life's inevitable changes gracefully. She met Beth the year before on a Sierra Club trip out west. They hit it off well. Well enough for Suzanna to ask if she could invite Beth on this trip. I trusted Suzanna's instincts and said, "Of course!"

Suzanna and Beth paired up as partners. We seemed to be the perfect foursome - fit and fabulous over-forty-some-things (okay, one of us well over forty and one well over fifty) who really enjoyed wilderness camping, paddling and the good company of like-minded women.

Brenda had no trouble finding the Okefenokee Restaurant, the only restaurant in Folkston at that time. The proprietors offered fine, down-home Southern fare. With the aromas of grilling ribs and charring hamburgers and frying chicken wafting out into the parking lot, I started salivating while Suzanna and Beth, both vegetarians, exchanged woe-is-me looks.

Okefenokee Restaurant

They knew the score though in the sleepy southern town and happily grazed, albeit selectively, on the buffet's offerings. I pointed out the macaroni and cheese, cole slaw, and desserts. The only items with no meat, meat chunk seasonings, or animal fat juices.

In stark contrast, Brenda and I chowed down voraciously on the golden-brown, crispy fried chicken, the ham seasoned collards, and the bacon-infused green beans. Both of those vegetables cooked to nearly unrecognizable form, just the way I prefer them. What a spread! Brenda and I levitated into carnivore nirvana, while Suzanna and Beth sunk smack dab into southern buffet herbivore hell.

We washed it all down with the delicious, sickly-sweet iced tea we southerners just refer to as tea. Every true southerner knows tea is really sweet ice tea. Just like I grew up slurping down at my grandmother's table. My mother did not allow us to have such sugary stuff. It would ruin our teeth and kidneys she said. That delicious sweet tea off my grandmother's table though easily qualified as dessert in and of itself, just like this Folkston Okefenokee Restaurant tea did.

Over lunch we became better acquainted and had a good time discovering bits and pieces of one another's lives. "Where were you born?" "Where have you lived?" "How long have you been living in Boston, Savannah, Big Pine, Indianapolis?" "Spouses?" "Children?" "Grand-children?" "Siblings?" "Profession?" The usual get-to-know-you questions.

Suzanna, originally from Pennsylvania, grew up in a Quaker household and boarded away at school from sixth grade through college, along with her younger sister Geri, also blessed with a magnificent mane of silvery springy curls. She married her high-school sweetheart and bore two sons. Their oldest, amazingly upbeat Sandy, hit by a car after chasing a ball into the street at age nine, and in spite of his persistent physical and mental challenges, bravely, boldly, humorously and quite happily embraced his life. He lived well into his late 30's. The scars of his accident however weighed heavily on the family, and eventually proved to be too much for Suzanna's marriage.

Suzanna's younger son Rob became a very successful professional financial manager and married Amy, a lovely young lady from the Bronx, giving Suzanna three smart, productive grandchildren. Suzanna, a career physical therapist, met a visiting Danish doctor Erik and remarried. She moved to his home in Copenhagen for a few years, but returned to the Boston area when that the relationship stopped working. She had recently lost Peter, a highly successful engineer and her loving companion of the last 17 years. She missed him terribly. He left her a gorgeous rural home and enough money to pay upkeep and annual taxes.

For many winters up until March 2020 when she sold the house, I visited Suzanna to snowshoe and cross-country ski. The house Peter left her abutted Groton Conservation Trust, and it was quite wonderful to just clip into snowshoes and shuffle out her front door with xc-skis strapped to our backs. We would bulldoze our way through deep snow downhill to the groomed trail, clip out of our snowshoes and into our xc-skis for over an hour. The temperatures could be quite frigid, and my thin southern heat-acclimated blood could only handle the cold for short periods, even though snowshoeing and xc-skiing warmed me up quickly.

Suzanna, 12 years my senior, stays quite fit by walking up and down hills and biking around her condo in Cambridge. I, from the flat coast of Georgia and specifically Tybee Island at sea level, am usually winded, when Suzanna is still gliding up the side of

Suzanna Black

a small mountain with no sign of stress. I stop many more times than she to gasp. My thighs protest the inclines, and my calves send messages to my brain that they are done long before the hike ends. Still, I manage to make it through each time. On the other end of the spectrum I have strong shoulders and can paddle for hours on end with no pain. I end up Paddling Miss Suzanna sort of like Driving Miss Daisy.

When watching sports with my father he would often comment on the "freaks of nature". He maintained that a highly successful super athlete separated from the rest of the pack because they were freaks of nature. Some part of their physical makeup enabled them to excel in their particular sport. My freak is my strong shoulders and upper arms. I really enjoy paddling. It is easy for me and relatively painless. Brenda's athletic freak is the same.

Brenda worked as a CPA and tax preparer in Naples.

Married a time or two, she produced no children. Now preferring to be single, she hung out with companions whenever the desire and/or opportunity presented itself. Mostly she enjoyed paddling and camping in the Glades with friends, male and female. Her two younger brothers live in California, and they all still grieved the recent loss of their beloved mother. Brenda moved her mother from the Midwest to Pine Island as her health failed. She regaled us with very funny Momma-in-Her-Dotage stories.

Beth, tall, ample figured, short blond hair, freckled Irish complexion, the youngest of us, had entered a Sisters of Mercy Convent right out of high school. She trained as a nurse to tend to the sick and dying. Five and a half years earlier she had met Patrick while on the job and fell madly, hopelessly in love. She left the safety of the convent to marry and enjoy three giddy years of wedded bliss before the onset of his devastating terminal illness. Dutifully she cared for him during the last two years of his life. Patrick had passed six months prior, and Suzanna hoped this trip might lift Beth's spirits.

I shared that I had always been the black sheep of my very conservative Southern Baptist family and followed my own path in all ways. I never found the peace nor solace in my parents' church that I did in nature, much to my mother's great angst. I spent as much time outside as allowed. Fortunately I grew up in a time when mothers let their children do just that. I had to be dragged inside to eat and bathe.

At this point, on my third marriage (it took me a while to get the hang of marriage) I served as an interpretive naturalist and educator. Or as I termed it, an ocean science translator for NOAA in Savannah at Gray's Reef National Marine Sanctuary. I had lived in a real treehouse with husband number two, a fellow naturalist and still a dear friend, Crawfish.

Now I lived in a house we simply called The Treehouse. My husband Chris, an electronics engineer, designed and built it, a treehouse on steroids so to speak, loaded with electronic and technological bells and whistles.

Happiest when in the Swamp or anywhere outdoors with friends and family, I had always been too busy to have children. I reasoned that over the many years of teaching I impacted more children than I could have ever done as a parent.

After paying the waitress/server/cook/cashier/multi-tasker, we thanked the manager (also her). Squeezing our overly stuffed selves into our two cars, we drove the seven miles to the Suwannee Canal Recreation Area to explore Chesser Island Homestead, walk the boardwalk and end our afternoon in the Owl's Roost Tower with its panoramic view of the prairie and sunset.

Later we'd head to Traders Hill Recreation Area and Campground for the night. A nice large park, maintained by Charlton County, set on the banks of the wild and scenic St. Mary's River. On weekends in nice weather it can be quite full of mostly very noisy locals enjoying tailgate parties.

Thankfully this evening we only needed to abide the long low whistles of the night trains interrupting our dreams as they made their way through the Folkston Funnel.

With the Atlantic to the east and the Okefenokee to the west, all eastern seaboard rails accommodating north-south bound trains are squeezed through the famed Folkston Funnel. Trains shoot through the funnel regularly 24/7 year round. Many train-watchers flock to Folkston just to watch the trains roll by on average every 20 minutes. Viewing platforms with speakers that pick up communication between railroad crews alert

Train in Folkston Funnel

enthusiasts to all approaching trains.

I reserved the Green Trail for this trip. In the morning our shuttle from Suwannee Canal Recreation Area would transport us up to our launch at Kingfisher Landing some 20 miles north. From there we would paddle seven miles to Bluff Lake through open gorgeous prairie. On our second day out we would cover nine miles from Bluff Lake to Floyd's Island mostly on winding trails through batteries lined with thick bushes – titi, sweetspire, and hurrah bush.

On the third day we were to paddle seven miles from Floyd's Island to Round Top through the lovely arched cypress entry way on the east side of the island and then through Grand Prairie. Our last night would be spent in the glory of Round Top that affords a 360° view of spectacular Grand Prairie. This is my favorite platform in the Swamp. Typically Sandhill Cranes come into the area to feed as the sun sets.

Throughout the night owls, mostly Barred, hoot incessantly and during the warm months the frog

Bluff Lake & Suwannee Canal Sign in Chase Praire on Blue Trail

chorus can be deafening. In spring gators bellow near and far. On our final day, we would paddle from Round Top through three miles of the Grand Prairie, and then nine miles down the Suwannee Canal back to the SCRA where our cars awaited us.

We left Brenda's car in the parking lot, and she climbed into my little white sporty 2002 Volvo station wagon for the drive to Chesser Island. The adventure began.

At our first stop an eight-foot mother gator and her young from nests over several years delighted us. She had some newbie eight-inch hatchlings from this year's nest. And a few one-footers from last year's brood, fewer two-footers from the year before, and only one or two three-footers from the year before that. We didn't notice any four-footers. Maybe as four year olds do, they had already left the protection of their maternal den.

Typically alligator nestlings stay near their mother's den

for protection until they disperse to establish their own territories. That typically happens at year four when about four-feet long. They rely on mother to protect them from predation by raccoons, possums, snakes, turtles, bobcats, herons, etc.

I once happened upon a Great Blue Heron snacking on hatchlings. Hard to watch, but I didn't interfere with Mother Nature. The next day, when I checked on the nest again, the former predator apparently ended up as mother's prey. Gray-blue feathers lay everywhere in configurations revealing the gruesome ending of the heron's good life. At least the Great Blue had a full belly, albeit of leathery scales.

Alligators tend to grow a foot a year until six years old; their growth rate slows after that. The yellow body bands of their youth fade and are only slightly visible around their tails. At around six they begin growing more in girth than in length. Females attain a maximum length of ten feet, but males continue to grow in length their entire lives, although slowly.

Next we stopped at the ditch along the way to marvel at the southern slender ladies' tresses. These delicate little white ground orchids have tiny bell-shaped flowers that spiral along the upper quarter of their long slender stems. I admire them for their beauty and hardiness. I cannot fathom how they survive while being so petite, delicate, and to my mind, completely vulnerable to wind, paws, feet, bugs, rain, you name it. Yet there they stood elegantly in their Lilliputian world. It's hard to believe they haven't found their way into a premium botanical shampoo yet.

We finally arrived at Chesser Homestead. Suzanna and I had explored here many times before, but this time was a first for Beth and Brenda. So we leisurely toured the cabin Tom and Ida Chesser built to raise

Southern Slender Ladies' Tresses Orchids *(Spiranthes lacera)*

their nine children in the late 1800's. In this area, as far as cabins go, it is a mansion with several bedrooms, a proper sitting room with a fireplace, and a kitchen with walk-in pantries and a large dining table with enough space for everyone, in particular a family of eleven, to sit down to eat at the same time. The large, wide porches accommodate swinging chairs up front and a bathtub with a hand-crank pump on the back side.

In the days before air conditioning, porches served as places to spend evenings catching cooling breezes, telling stories, and playing music. Some folks even slept out there when really hot and the breeze stiff enough to blow away bugs.

Every time I visit Chesser Homestead and see that hand-cranked pump on the back porch spilling water into the claw-foot bathtub, I am reminded of my own early childhood visits to my grandparents' farm. My mother grew up in an era when rural North Carolina was not connected to the public water system nor sewage nor garbage pickup nor electricity. Electricity did not come to my grandparents' very rural farm until I was at least ten in 1961. Soon after that, an electric pump on the well magically provided running water. Up until that point I bathed in the kitchen sink with water pumped from the only hand pump in the house or out in the barn in a washtub as my grandfather continued to do even when indoor plumbing finally came to the farm.

The Refuge even built an exact replica of the facility better known as the outhouse or privy. Seeing that small

Tub and Hand Water Pump at Chesser Cabin

but very essential building also evokes memories, some humorous, some not so.

Before indoor plumbing at my grandparent's house while answering the call of nature in the middle of the night, I encountered one too many close calls with cows, pigs, raccoons, etc. I loved the little wild raccoons and possums but the enormous cows and dangerous hogs rightfully frightened the bejesus out of me. I took to using the chamber pot my mother used her entire life while on the farm. As disgusting as it was to me, I found it preferable to the would-be dangerous night-time trips to the privy.

In the middle of the day however, the emptied and sanitized chamber pot returned to its hiding place under the bed, out of sight, not to be used except under cover of night. During daylight, the odorous, ominous privy had to be abided.

At age seven, skinny and small, I did not adequately cover the adult-sized holes in the two-holed outhouse, ergo the term "two-holer." My bottom covered perhaps one quarter of one wide gaping circle. To be safe, I employed a two-handed hold on either side of the deep, dark hole, propping myself up sort of like a two-legged tripod. Not really stable, but the best I could manage.

One hot afternoon, distracted by buzzing bugs, I reflexively released one hand to shoo them off. Big problem. I lost balance instantly, nearly dropping heinie-first through that dark smelly, steaming, stinky, godawful hole. I panicked but quickly saved myself from certain death. I do believe that day initiated the honing of my quick eye-hand reflexes. Pure survival, I'm telling you, pure survival.

To this day, on nights after particularly stressful work, I dream of that incident. I awake in a cold sweat, sit

Chris Morris at Chesser Cabin

bolt upright with both hands firmly planted on either side of my rear end, clutching the bedsheets. My chest heaves in deep breaths. I cringe and shudder at the very thought of how I almost ended up. I am forever grateful to Mr. Crapper for inventing his wonderful new-fangled flusher.

Chesser Homestead, recreated to depict life around the Swamp in the 1850's, closely resembles the way my grandparents' farm looked up until the early 1960's. It has a smokehouse that still smells of curing smoke, a functional corn crib, a fenced garden growing seasonal vegetables and tall, willowy strap-leafed sugar cane and a shed for cane grinding and boiling. It even has beehives made from hollowed-out cypress log sections.

On the south side of the house, in the neatly swept white-sand yard, stand a deep well and a sharpening stone wheel. Out front a display tells of turpentining.

Extracting resin from pine trees to make turpentine was and still is a very sticky business and undertaken only in warm months when the sap runs freely, and also when rattlesnakes are active.

The swept yards serve two purposes. First and foremost is to provide a barrier to fire. Since the structures of that time period were made of heart pine to discourage indigenous subterranean termites, they were and still are veritable tinder boxes. A wide barrier of swept sand offers an excellent fire break. Secondly a swept yard discourages vermin – snakes, bugs, unwelcome visitors of any species – offering no hiding place. Holly branches stripped of leaves and bundled together served as yard

Swamp Island Drive Boardwalk to Owl's Roost Tower

brooms. The youngest members of the family swept the yard.

From there we moved on to the boardwalk, one of my favorite places. Exploring the prairie via boardwalk, on foot, makes transecting the peat easy and painless. You don't get wet nor bogged down.

From the boardwalk, only three feet above the surface of the prairie, you can see a lot of swamp life up close. Typically green anoles and fence lizards scurry from the top of the boards to hide underneath, gripping the irregularities of those surfaces with their well-adapted, Sperry Top Sider like soled toes. Hatchling alligators are safely observed even with their super protective mother close by. Through binoculars you see the details of color in feathers and beaks and legs of herons, egrets, and Sandhill Cranes (the Florida subspecies year-round, and the Greater subspecies as a winter visitor). I marvel at the sharp delineation of zones, bands, stripes, bars, etc. made by – think about it – overlapping feathers. Marvelous!

Also observed from the boardwalk is a jungle of vegetation: maiden cane, broom sedge, titi, sweetspire, greenbriar, hurrah bush, sphagnum moss, cypress, black gum, cinnamon and chain ferns, wax myrtle, hollies, etc. Just lots to see here.

We ambled along the nearly mile-long boardwalk, stopping often to enjoy the sights and discuss their importance. We were having such a good time. Easy, natural companions, our conversation flowed comfortably and freely.

At the end of the boardwalk, the 45-feet tall observation platform called the Owl's Roost Tower looms large. Barred and Great Horned Owls roost here, ergo the name; maybe diminutive Screech Owls too. As you climb the stairs, the tower sways a bit and can make some people a bit nervous. I recall Beth commenting on how she found the gentle sway quite relaxing. We looked here and there as we climbed, regularly exclaiming, "Oooohhh, look, over there at that handsome Great Blue!" "Hey, do y'all see the Sandhills over this way?" "I think I see a Roseate Spoonbill over there! Yep, it's a Rosie!" Lots of birds dotted the surrounding prairie.

After we summited Owl's Roost, other visitors trickled up, joining us on the spacious deck. At first everyone quietly spoke in whispers so as not to disturb anyone else's reverie while viewing the wildlife.

The panoramic view from the Owl's Roost is quite stunning. To the west, south and east the prairie sprawls flat and watery, punctuated with low shrubs of titi, hurrah bush and sweetspire. Wax myrtle and hollies find foothold on higher ground. Off in the distance cypress standing in their domes silhouette a gently rolling tree line. Large birds in the distance

Owl's Roost Tower

Spotting Scope at Owl Roost Tower

easily identified are often difficult to see well enough
to pick out details even with a pair of excellent binoculars.
The Refuge provides a high-power spotting scope
attached to the tower's top level railing. It provides a
surprisingly clear view of far off objects even though it
is subjected to year-round weather. It is well designed,
made of exceptionally durable metal with high quality
glass lenses.

Back to the north, the direction we came, you look
back over the boardwalk into the cypress dome you
just walked through. I have observed small tree frogs,
squirrel and gray and piney woods tree frogs to be
exact at eye level. The higher level branches of the
cypress surrounding the tower are right there. You
can reach out and touch them. The frogs can be right
there. The males calling their little horny hearts out

82

after an afternoon's quick shower advertising their "stuff".

Our four-way conversation continued for us very sociable females. A peaceful place brings out peaceful conversation and leads to introspection.

Eventually our talk turned a bit more personal. I knew Suzanna still struggled in settling Peter's affairs since his passing. I ventured to ask, "Suzanna, have you been able to deal with Peter's ashes yet?"

Since we had been discussing Peter on the way down in the car, I felt comfortable in asking this of her in front of Beth and Brenda. They both had shared recent deaths in their lives too.

"You know, he's still in the closet, but I talk to him almost every day. Since he passed right before Thanksgiving, the ground was too frozen to bury him. And besides, his sister and son couldn't come back so soon after they were with us during his transitioning. Every now and again I hear him call to me, telling me he needs to be in the ground and not in the closet. So in a few months, when the ground thaws and Holly and Nick can get back east, we'll celebrate his life and bury his ashes. In the meantime, he's in the closet just a while longer."

I noticed the other folks sharing Owl's Roost turned their heads in our direction as a gesture of support I guessed. Perhaps they had experienced similar situations.

Brenda chimed in, "Yeah, I know how that goes. My mother came to live with me the last few years of her life, and we had a really good time, especially considering she wasn't in her own home but in mine. My two younger brothers promised to take Momma to Las Vegas, but she died before that happened. So they insisted I send her anyway, her ashes that is, so they could take her to

View from Top Level of Owl's Roost Tower

Vegas as promised."

The other folks on Owl's Roost pretended to keep to their bird watching but now inched in a bit closer to our little group of gaggling girls. We tittered and giggled, really enjoying one another's stories at this point. Apparently, our eavesdroppers enjoyed them too, but they still feigned to quietly look at the panoramic view.

"So you sent your mom to your brothers via the US Postal Service?" I asked.

"Yep, it wasn't all that hard. No one asked the contents of my package and I didn't volunteer to reveal them either. I did attest that it didn't contain any dangerous chemicals nor explosives nor whatever it is they ask. The ashes didn't fall into any of those categories. So off to California Momma flew, courtesy of the United States Postal Service."

Beth joined in, "I can just imagine the gasp of a postal worker if that box had met with an accident and had to be opened. Wouldn't they've been surprised?!"

We all laughed perhaps a bit too loudly, and so did some of our eavesdroppers. Their laughs though quieter and more muted, so as not to let on that they were actually listening in. I knew better by now.

Brenda continued, "Yeah, my brothers are a pair of jokers all right. They put Momma in a daypack and took her to all of the shows and casinos they'd promised her. I'm sure she enjoyed every minute of it!"

My active imagination sped to Vegas. I could just see Brenda's brothers holding up her urn for a better view of Wayne Newton at Caesars or of Siegfried and Roy's lion show at the Mirage. What a hoot!

"So where's Momma now?" Suzanna politely asked.

"My brothers sprinkled her in a few places around Vegas and then mailed her back to me. I've sprinkled her in the Gulf of Mexico and in the Atlantic and on South Beach in Miami. She really loved that place. Whenever we went there, we ate almost always at Puerto Sagua. Momma's finally at rest. Just in a lot of places!" Brenda chuckled. All of us did too, including our eavesdroppers.

"Brenda, you were very thoughtful in honoring your mother so lovingly", I said. "You honored her wishes respectfully. I heard of a guy who honored his friend's wishes but not so respectfully. A dying man made his friend promise to spread his ashes in ballparks across the country and so he did. He got a bit lazy though and instead of spreading them on the infields as specified, he killed two birds with one stone he reported by flushing his friend down the toilet when he answered the call of nature."

That brought about the intended response. All of us guffawed. The others on the platform choked and snickered loudly. Not so subtle eavesdroppers now.

Suzanna, perhaps a bit too directly in her New England way, asked Beth about her husband. "Beth, what've you done with Patrick?"

Beth looked away. The light-heartedness of the past few moments drained from her face. The pain of her loss still intense. In a moment she looked back and said softly, "He's with me. He always will be."

We weren't quite sure what she meant. Suzanna continued supportively, "Well, we know he'll always be with you and you with him. You two had such an incredibly strong bond in your short time together."

Wetlands on Swamp Island Boardwalk

Beth brightened. "I know, it really was quite special. We met, and that was that. I didn't have any hesitation about leaving the convent at all. Most of my sisters strongly supported me. Mother Superior, not so much. Patrick was my life, my love, my destiny, my entire world."

Our eavesdroppers shifted body positions, twisting our way, reacting to Beth's revelation, her confession, of being a former nun. Eddies of conversation rippled quietly among the three or four smaller groups crowding in around us to hear. Checking with each other to confirm what they had just heard.

Beth continued unprompted now, moved to share. "My dearest, darling Patrick is so special to me I decided we shall never be apart. He will become me, and I him."

Rather cryptic but appropriately metaphorical, we all thought for a deeply grieving widow, a former spiritual woman of habit, a nun.

"He's with me even now." Her fingers automatically clutched the glass bauble with his entombed ashes that hung around her neck.

Gator on Log

Brenda, Suzanna, and I sighed in understanding. Visibly relaxed at her explanation, our furrowed brows smoothed. Relieved that her unusual comment wasn't something more eccentric, more out there, well, more than it could have been.

The others strained to sneak a peek at her neck. The three of us marveled at the artistry of the lovely teardrop-shaped glass pendant with the gray ashes inside. How do they do that? Were those really Patrick's ashes?

Beth went on, "Patrick is right on my bedside table too. Every night I tell him what I did during the day and how much I miss him and what we'll do when we're together again. I miss him so very much."

She was looking down now, her eyes welling up with tears.

We drew into her pain and anguish. Each of us viscerally channeling her emotions.

Beth went on, adding nonplussed, "Each night, I wet my little finger and dip it into his ashes and then put his dear sweet ashes into my mouth. He will always be a part of me." She smiled sweetly.

With her last words still hanging in the air, Suzanna, Brenda, and I uncontrollably flinched. I think I actually wretched.

Hundreds of needles loudly scratched across hundreds of vinyl disks amplified through an enormous wall of speakers.

Millions of long finger nails screeched down thousands of chalky blackboards.

The eavesdroppers gasped and visibly recoiled. No polite sensitive subtlety there.

They tittered and snorted in stunned derision. Everyone

Stairs of Owl's Roost Tower

loudly talking now. The heretofore curious but considerate crowd erupted into a rude buzz.

"What'd she say?" "Can you believe that?" "Oh * My * God!"

I finally broke in with what I hoped would lighten the atmosphere, "Well, that's one way to keep him with you....always!"

I swallowed hard, trying not to betray any emotion, highly uncomfortable.

My mind raced. It would take a while to digest. No, that's no good. Vegetarianism. Daily requirements of minerals. Thoughts in bad taste. No, that's no good either. Stop! Help! Get me off this tower!

I wanted to say something to comfort Beth but couldn't come up with anything, nothing at all. For once in my life, at a loss for words.

I wanted to inspect her teeth for any ashes that might still be sticking to them. Oh Dear God! Stop that. Don't go there.

Instead I moved towards the steps, sincerely hoping that, going down, the swaying tower would again somehow comfort Beth.

From the bottom of the stairs I looked up to watch Beth descend. I swear she had her head on Patrick's shoulder as they walked arm in arm. She smiled serenely.

So what was the rest of the trip going to reveal?

I wondered if each of us would talk about artifacts we cherished of our dearly departed ones.

What is held dear from a loved who didn't leave anything behind except the emptiness of arms that no longer hold you tight nor lips that no longer wet yours?

Beth seemed to have gotten it right. She kept what she needed of Patrick. He would be with her always.

Great Egret on Swamp Island Drive Boardwalk

CHAPTER 4

Swamp Goddess Emerges

Suwanee Canal Run Platform

November 1979 and 1980

M y darling pair of Dr. Bobs sipped wine at their
campsite, unwinding after Day One in the
Okefenokee Swamp. They were repeat customers
whom I had led on trips for a few years in a row.
Clearly something about the wild Okefenokee captured
their imaginations.

They didn't look like outdoorsmen nor natural
buddies. One balding, tanned, loud, and pleasingly
plump. The other wan, wrinkled, wispy, and quiet. I
guessed that their medical backgrounds made them
the easy companions they seemed to be.

They were two of twelve guests on our three-day
canoeing adventure. This first day we had paddled
eleven miles down Canal Run on the eastern side of the
famous sprawling Swamp. It had been a good workout
but not too hard of a paddle, and now, we relaxed and
savored the day's accomplishments.

The Okefenokee covers about 700 square miles, running approximately 35 miles north to south and approximately 20 miles east to west in the southeastern corner of Georgia. The Okefenokee National Wildlife Refuge regulates most of the 438,000 acres it encompasses. The largest cypress swamp in the world, it hosts the planet's largest population of American Alligators, well over 10,000.

Black Bear, Sandhill Cranes, and Wood Storks are also significant megafauna in the complex ecosystem. The Okefenokee is a wonderful wilderness area that has a long history of use and abuse. And now, thankfully, redemption.

My personal relationship, my love affair, with the Okefenokee began after I graduated from Armstrong State College in 1976. In the fall of that year I began leading trips into this hallowed place, and it became to me a real wilderness home.

The two Dr. Bobs were regular guests on my trips, and they religiously planned their schedules every November for Okefenokee trips I led. By this trip, I had led nearly 100 multiple-night trips into this wild place that I simply call "The Swamp."

I was truly flattered when the director of our small non-profit school of the outdoors Wilderness Southeast told me that, when the Dr. Bobs made their reservations, they always wanted to be assured specifically I would be the leader.

One of my traditions as a wilderness hostess is to treat our campers to some good red wine at the end of each day, best served room temperature in metal Sierra cups, not fine crystal.

And so I made my customary rounds and, as a nod to our history together, visited the Dr. Bobs first. As I got within earshot of them, I got snippets of an unusual

Mallory Pearce - Artist, Calligrapher, Animator, and Naturalist with His Vision of Swamp Goddess

conversation.

"Well, did you get a glimpse of the Swamp Goddess today? Or were you paddling too hard?" I overheard tan Dr. Bob say.

"Oh, yeah, in all her glory. Like a nymph in the water hyacinths," rejoined wan Dr. Bob in a dreamy tone.

"I'm going to try and tape her siren song. It's like all the swamp creatures know her. We sure are lucky to be here."

I didn't bother to process it right then. I moved on to other campers, giving them the red-wine treat. Mostly they were recounting the sights and sounds of the day, talking about the gorgeous changing of the feathery green Cypress needles to autumnal russet brown.

Cypress and Larch, also known as Tamarack, are the only indigenous deciduous conifers we have in Georgia, and in North America for that matter.

Earlier in the day our Swampers thrilled at sighting

94

two sleepy Barred Owls sitting trance-like in different Cypress trees along the canal, Red Shouldered Hawks screeching high up, and squadrons of Turkey and Black Vultures soaring in lazy circles overhead.

One couple commented that the Dr. Bobs were in their own private world. I joked that I couldn't tell them much because of guide-client privilege but that their conversations were always interesting to be sure.

In fact, I smiled ear to ear seeing them yet again. Their contrasting looks mirrored their contrasting personalities. Tan Dr. Bob began his career as a general practitioner in private practice. But halfway through raising his three children, he changed course. Feeling that he did not have enough time for his kids nor for his wife, he took a hospital job as an anesthesiologist with better hours and a more manageable schedule.

Wan Dr. Bob, an epidemiologist, spent much of his time in a lab staring into a microscope at virulent bacteria. He was quiet where his counterpart was boisterous. Circumspect while his odd colleague overbearing. His wit dry, while the other laughed readily at his own sometimes witty, mostly lame, puns.

I liked them as a pair. I had come to know each as a seasoned professional who took his job seriously. Each completely dedicated to his patients and profession for the greater good of humanity. I stay up to date in First Aid and CPR, but it's always good to have a doctor in the house and certainly on a wilderness trip.

I passed their campsite again, and, beyond the wall of palmettos, I could clearly hear them, now sounding like they were discussing a scientific paper. Tan Bob wound up.

"You're right about that. You don't see latissimus dorsi like that except in museum sculptures or textbook drawings."

"The way she moves, you can't tell if she's a creature of land or water. How old can she be?"

"I'd say ageless. I couldn't keep my eyes off her clavicles," gushed Wan Bob.

After finishing my first round of wine service and ongoing debriefing with the other campers, I made my way again to the odd couple. I still puzzled over their "Swamp Goddess" story. She didn't figure into any Okefenokee tale that I had heard. And neither Bob seemed like a New Age type.

The only Swamp story I knew of anyone with a regal title was Miss Lydia Smith, Queen of the Okefenokee, Miss Lydie to family and friends. Miss Lydie is my all-time favorite Swamp character. She is worth looking up to understand just how much she

Dipping for Critters Under the Lily Pads

defied the norms of the time for her gender to become a most successful business woman with only six days of formal schooling. She amassed a fortune of over a million dollars by the time of her death in January 1938. Her fortune began with the one cow and one sow her father had given her.

She married twice. Both times to hired help. Her first marriage lasted 23 years. A year or two after the death of Gordon Stone another much younger man caught her eye. He like the first held her appreciation and respect for the land. J. Melton Crews, Baby Doll to Miss Lydie, worked the land as she worked it. Soon they became engaged, he at 21 and she 63. A year later they married.

Their story is memorable enough and made even more memorable when Miss Lydie negotiated the release of Baby Doll from a 20-year murder sentence. The murder could have been an accident as Crews

Cathy with Beloved Bent-Shaft Ash Paddle (Photo by Bryan Schroeder)

maintained, but the local constabulary assessed the incident differently.

After learning that Baby Doll had been mistreated in prison though, the sheriff disappeared. Curiously no one ended up being charged in the shooting. Shortly thereafter Miss Lydie and her lawyer went to Atlanta to bribe a "high official" with $10,000 for the release of Baby Doll. Miss Lydie, Baby Doll and the lawyer returned to Charlton County and stopped at the bank before going home. Miss Lydie needed to cancel the check for the $10,000. With Baby Doll home, his record marked served, the high official had no recourse but to eat his loss and say nothing.

The Dr. Bobs were still at it when I approached. "My paddling partner couldn't figure why I wanted to keep so close to her, and he kept telling me to ease off. But finally he got it and became completely transfixed too. Then he paddled just as hard as me to keep her in view at the perfect angle."

What? Had Miss Lydie made an appearance?

Wan Bob caught sight of me out of the corner of his eye, looked startled, and shushed Tan Bob. They stopped talking completely, which meant they weren't conversationally adept enough to jump to another topic appropriate for my ears.

I poured their wine picking up on their uncomfortable, embarrassed tongue-tied silence. They stood frozen like two Docs in headlights.

"So", I began inquisitively, "I just overheard you talking about a Swamp Goddess. Did you mean Queen, as in Queen of the Okefenokee, Miss Lydia Smith?"

Instead of eagerly jumping right on that open invitation to tell that story like I expected outgoing and talkative Tan Bob would do, they both turned scarlet. Well, actually,

Wan Dr. Bob turned scarlet, while Tan Dr. Bob, having a pigment head start, turned the most amazingly beautiful shade of plum. They both stared down at their feet and uncomfortably shuffled in the white sand covered with fresh chestnut-brown autumn leaf litter.

I pushed again, "Okay, in all of my time in the Swamp listening to others interpret and tell her history and reading old and new publications, never once have I heard tell of a Swamp Goddess. So you two are going to have to tell me your story. I want to tell her story too."

"Ah, well, let's see, er, you tell her," stammered Wan Bob passing off to Tan Bob.

"Well, uh, well", choked Tan Bob.

I wrinkled my nose and cocked my head. "Wait. Ohhhhh. Am I the Swamp Goddess?" I said it in disbelief, but their verbal paralysis led me only to that logical conclusion.

My two dear Dr. Bobs like outed school boys sheepishly nodded their heads.

After what to them I am sure seemed an eternity, a very amused and pleased smile spread across my face. "I love it! I'll take it!" I shouted. I warmly embraced my two heretofore secret admirers individually. And then, giggling, we hugged as three, like a small secret society.

Group hugs were another custom typically saved for the end of each of my trips. This one, a bit ahead of schedule.

Tan Bob, exuberantly turned to the group, "Excuse me! Excuse me! Your attention please!" When he had everyone's attention, he held up his super-sized Sierra cup of wine and pronounced in true thespian voice, "Hear Ye, Hear Ye, and Hear Ye. I present to you our newly publically anointed Swamp Goddess!"

Swamp Goddess Sleepwear Fashion Statement (Photo by Theresa Wexler)

He bent in a deep respectful bow and led off, "All Hail Swamp Goddess! All Hail Swamp Goddess! All Hail Swamp Goddess!" The chanting went on for several minutes as I curtsied in every direction and basked in the glory of the moment.

Without knowing it, I had been their secret Swamp Goddess for four years. But now, henceforth, I would own the title and rule over my realm proudly. I had not promoted the title, nor asked for it, but now I embraced it.

Their adoration came about from my normal exercise routine. Between canoeing trips I lifted weights to be fit enough to endure long, grueling paddling days on open waterways, often into strong winds and most of the

Swamp Goddess in Her Realm (Photo by Andy Collins)

time with an inexperienced bow partner who usually outweighed me by a considerable amount.

It is the responsibility of a leader to take the least experienced and weakest paddler. My weight-lifting routine and many years of paddling had given me the back muscles the good Doctors so admired.

I wear almost no sunscreen because my system is very sensitive to chemicals. Instead, I wear a bathing suit underneath lightweight long-sleeved shirts and quick-drying long pants. On canoe trips in warm months, before 10:00 and after 3:00, I typically shed my outer layers to let my skin breathe and to soak up the sun's natural vitamin D. I always wear hat and sunglasses throughout the day.

The very next year, like migrating seasonal visitors, my two darling Dr. Bobs arrived again, as they would for the next six years. Sometimes they brought their teen and adult children along to experience the wonders of the Okefenokee, the Swamp they unequivocally adored.

This year however the Swamp Goddess had a surprise for them.

On our first day, we paddled the Red Trail, 12 miles, one of the longest trail segments in the Swamp. On flat, still dark water our canoes wended along the sinuous trail through fragrant white water lily pads, past long slender blades of blue flag iris and numerous peat blowups delicately bristling with rose-colored sundews.

We reached Maul Hammock platform just before sunset. My co-leader Jim and I helped everyone out of their canoes, and then unloaded the group's common gear and personal gear.

Jim set up the kitchen to cook dinner, and I set about the platform with the much-anticipated first aliquot of evening wine. The two Dr. Bobs had paddled with their children, so had not been in close contact with each other the entire day until now. They were recounting the day's activities and comparing their predictable notes.

"You know the sun was really intense today, and I was afraid Swamp Goddess wasn't going to do her thing," said Tan Bob.

"Well, you know it's good that she's so mindful of sunburn since she's in the sun all the time. She told me before that she doesn't like to wear sunscreen because she can taste it on her tongue, a strong indication she's very sensitive to any type of chemical. I know she doesn't use bug spray either," added Wan Bob.

I was flattered that the conversant pair involved themselves with my personal health strategies. They were after all physicians. I held out the wine bottle, and they reflexively held out their Sierra cups, suspiciously larger than anyone else's.

"So, did your Swamp Goddess deliver today?" I asked.

"Oh, yes! You...er...she is in fine form this year!" stumbled Tan Bob.

I shook my head and said, "I hate to differ with you good doctors, but Swamp Goddess hasn't appeared quite yet."

They both knitted their brows, cocked their heads, and looked puzzled.

As they swirled their nightly ration of wine in their aluminum cups I said, "Hold that thought, gentlemen! And stay right here."

I nodded to Jim, who had been awaiting my cue. We both disappeared into our respective tents. A few minutes later, still inside his tent, he called out in his most courtly voice, "My Lady, are you yet ready, My Lady, Swamp Goddess?"

"Why yes, my Consort. I am ready, anon!" I said as eloquently as I could.

Jim emerged from his tent wearing an "onesie" nylon tuxedo complete with cummerbund and bow tie. His tux showed not one wrinkle even though it had been balled up in his small duffle bag all day long. He took position at the entrance to my tent, the consummate courtly consort.

Jim Bitler in His Realm on Ossabaw Island

The eyes of the two Dr. Bobs were riveted in our direction, and they motioned the other campers to stop talking and pay attention. I waited for anticipation to build. Then like a beautiful butterfly from the confines of her cocoon, I emerged my low-profile tent in a flowing long gown. Shrimp pink with chic spaghetti straps, elegantly falling in Greek toga-style folds.

The effect perfect. Audible gasps turned into delighted laughter. My repurposed bridesmaid gown began a new life. First worn at my sister-in-law's wedding; now at the Dr. Bobs' presentation ceremony.

On Jim's courtly arm, I floated in bare feet to the middle of the platform, my hair artfully mussed from the confines of my tiny tent.

Jim twirled me around and around to the delighted guffaws of our guests. Their applause reverberated off the surrounding Cypress trees. Their delighted laughter

Sylvia Cross - Artist, Teacher, and Spiritual Guru with Her Vision of Swamp Goddess

echoed across the Swamp. Swamp Goddess reveled in their adoration.

The Dr. Bobs beamed like proud fathers at a coming-out party.

Swamp Goddess had finally emerged in all of her glory!

All eyes focused on my clavicles.

*P*ostscript:

Beginning with that trip and on every trip since, I pack my Swamp Goddess gown which changed over the years. And on every overnight trip into my great watery realm I reveal my true identity.

By the mid 80's the two Dr. Bobs stopped coming on my trips together.

I never heard from Dr. Bob Noble of Kentucky

again after his last trip together with Dr. Bob Harris in the mid 80's.

Dr. Bob Harris of Knoxville, Tennessee continued to paddle with me until just a year or so before his death in 2008. My remembrance of him is at the end of "Swan Song of the Swamp".

My friend, co-leader and colleague Jim Bitler died way too young in April 2011 on a Sunday afternoon while taking a nap in his trailer on Ossabaw Island. He was 55. On his lap that fateful day were his two Boston terriers, Beau ("that's Beau-regardless," he always explained) and Kate ("Katherine the Great").

On his answering machine you would hear him say, "If I don't answer, chances are I am somewhere on this beautiful island loving my job." Bitler, accompanied by Beau and Kate, greeted visitors to Ossabaw at the dock where he would load them in his truck, drive them to their quarters and start the magic. Through him, the island's history came alive. He was a scientist, raconteur and naturalist. He is greatly missed. May You Rest in Everlasting Peace, Jim.

CHAPTER 5

Big Hand

Mixon's Hammock

Fall 1985

I have to admit, working with kids has not always been my forte. My language does not always resonate with the wee ones. I use too many multisyllabic words and give somewhat detailed explanations for natural history phenomena. Internally I struggle for just the right words and just the right tone and most of the time when I really try I get it right. I just have to remember to substitute words, like number two for defecation.

With older kids, middle and high school aged and especially college, I find it much easier. All I have to do is drift into discussion of sex strategies and scatology, and I am golden. They become proverbial putty in my hands, hanging on every word.

Because we were short on staff, I agreed to co-lead an Okefenokee trip for a group of third graders from a private school in Atlanta, the Paidea School. Paidea enjoyed an excellent reputation as a progressive, cutting-edge alternative school with teachers employing creative educational protocol, methodology and techniques.

I don't know exactly what those techniques were, but, sure enough, those kids were most enjoyable and quite intellectually superior to many adults I have encountered. Whatever those teachers exposed their students to in the classrooms, carried over to their field trips, making them most enjoyable to us trip leaders.

Lori, the lead teacher, had a mass of sandy-colored curls cascading over her shoulders and spilling down her back. She sported freckles and a winning smile. Her students adored her not because of her wholesome good looks but because she made learning fun. She did hands-on activities with them to underscore a new concept. She encouraged them to investigate whatever part of the new concept sparked their interest. She rewarded, congratulated, and guided her charges. Expertly, effortlessly, she inspired all who observed her to become a better teacher, educator, guide. And she could tell a heck of a good story.

She let me know right off the bat that she wanted to

Canoe Party Lands on Mixon Hammock

tell ghost stories around the campfire. I voiced strong unequivocal opposition.

While I didn't claim to know the psyche of a child all that well, I did remember being one myself and remembered being uncomfortable and even fearful of unfamiliar places. I knew being in a wild place might evoke natural fears.

As a child I spooked easily. Most likely a result of having an older tormenting brother who delighted in telling me awful things just before bedtime. My own child mind worked overtime at night, bringing monsters into my bedroom that waited for just the right moment for me to dangle my feet over the side of my bed. Or perhaps, because I forgot to check the closet before going to bed, a goblin hid there until I drifted off to sleep and then would "get" me. I certainly didn't think these kids needed any more fuel to fan the flames of already healthy active imaginations.

Anyway, I resolved that telling a ghost story to these kids around the campfire would not happen on my watch. I let Lori know that way ahead of time when we were planning this trip.

The first day of the trip finally arrived warm and sunny for fall. The kids were wound up from riding the bus for five hours, so, when they hit the ground, they raced around the parking lot like whirling dervishes. I got dizzy watching them. Their teachers Lori, Jock, Martha, Elise, Pedro, and Rubin didn't notice. They let them run with abandon. Better to let them run off their energy, although they were sure going to need some for canoeing to our campsite.

My co-leader Kimba and I had a quiet ride down from Savannah, so the noise and activity level of the kids already overloaded our senses. Their energy pure and raw. All good though, all good.

Billy's Lake Fall Colors

Lori conferred with us about the plan for the afternoon. The other five teachers nodded as a unit in total agreement. Lori, Martha, and Pedro were seasoned veterans, having gone on several trips with us before. They knew the ropes. The others were neophytes to the school and to camping.

Kimba gathered the kids around her and had them eating out of her hand in no time. She talked "kid" really well. In short order she had paddling partners paired up, with the tiniest kids paired with adults. For this large class we brought 12 canoes of our own and rented a few more from Stephen Foster State Park. We would be camping on Mixon's Hammock tucked into the southern pocket of Billy's Lake for two nights.

In November the nights are chilly and the days relatively warm. It's very pleasant and quite a lovely time to be in the Okefenokee.

Kimba and I gathered up our diminutive paddlers for a safety briefing and to go over paddling methods and etiquette.

The nice thing about kids is they catch on quickly. The

canoes with only kids paddling them did very well. Their light body weights and the small amount of gear we entrusted to their 17.5' canoes distributed their overall weight to nearly nothing allowing their canoes to skim the surface like fallen leaves blown by a gentle breeze.

We paddled the short distance, three miles or so, from Stephen Foster State Park south on Billy's Lake to Mixon's Hammock.

The wind at our backs pushed us along nicely. I pulled out my purple umbrella like Mary Poppins for an extra lift from the wind and for comic relief. The kids howled, and the teachers snapped photos. What a most pleasant afternoon on the lake!

Cypress needles were just turning russet, under-going senescence (drop off) with the approach of winter. Cypress and larch (aka tamarack) are the only conifers (cone-bearing trees) in North America that drop their needles in the fall. All other conifers are evergreen, dropping and replacing their needles as needed throughout the year.

Swamp Goddess Deploying Umbrella Spinnaker in Billy's Lake (Photo by Andre Turner)

Some of the russet brown cypress needles already beautifully carpeted the surface of the black mirrored water. Most catkins (the male pollen-bearing tassels) still clung to the upper branches like frilly Christmas tree ornaments. The small baby fist-sized cones had already dropped off the lower branches. If they fell on dry peat, seeds inside the cones might germinate and begin growing into new cypresses, knees and all.

Every half mile or so a vividly bright canary-yellow cluster of tickseed sunflowers swayed in the gentle breeze. Just gorgeous. I snapped off a lot of pictures using my SLR Pentax with color slide film. The kids paddled admirably. A few zigzagged here and there, but mostly they steered a true course for Mixon's Hammock. I encouraged them to paddle close to the left side of Billy's Lake to catch the afternoon sun, but not too close.

In the shallow water next to the trees, it's easy to be upended by a submerged log or cypress knee. High water levels, as now, cover some of the knees close to the water's edge and can be particularly insidious submerged hazards. You can't see them, and your canoe can teeter on them until you either dislodge or flip. We didn't want kids playing canoe see-saw and certainly not flipping.

Why cypress trees have knees has been long debated. Knees are soft woody projections that grow above the normal water level at a nearly right angle to the outward growing lateral roots. Current thinking is that they may serve two functions.

The function most agree on is that the knees provide support and stabilization.

Cypresses growing in swamps tend to be buttressed with prominent knees. Some knees I have observed are over six feet high. By contrast, cypresses growing

Mixon's Hammock Landing

in well-drained areas exhibit very little buttressing. In a dry habitat they have reduced knees or as in some places, no knees at all. They just don't need the support since the soil is firm enough and provides excellent purchase for the roots.

A cautionary observation that I share with adults is this, if you are looking at buying bottomland and the tree trunks have swollen bases, be sure to come back after a hard rain. Most likely you will find that the land is under water at certain times of the year. If you are not averse to canoeing or motor-boating home during those times, then it may be a good purchase for you. Just be sure to build your house on deep-seated stilts, high enough to withstand a 100-year flood.

The other function cypress knees may serve is providing oxygen to the roots as pneumatophores (gas exchanging devices). Since cypress tend to grow in waters with low dissolved oxygen, this function would be helpful. However, there is little actual evidence to support this function. In one study, swamp cypress with their knees removed continued to thrive. Further, laboratory tests demonstrated that the knees were not effective at depleting oxygen in a sealed chamber. Nonetheless the function is still posited, so I state it with my best Swamp Goddess disclaimer.

Mixon is an old Swamper name. My friends the Griffis family live just outside the Okefenokee National Wildlife Refuge boundary. They have lived in this same location on the banks of the Suwannee River since the 1850's. Many generations of Mixon's have hunted, fished, loved, died and served as ferrymen on this land. The earliest generation set up a homestead here because it was the narrowest place to ford the Suwannee River. They could easily pole a bateau to ferry people, their animals, goods, and gear across the river.

Some generations down the decades, in the mid 1940's, very young and pretty Alice Howell married older, well-established Lem Griffis, whose mother was a Mixon. They eventually begat two sons, Alpin and Arden, and two daughters, Maldine and Mary Alice. Tall, lanky well-spoken Lem provided well for his family as a fishing and hunting guide into the famous Okefenokee. His lovely young wife began cooking for his clients, some very famous. She cooked so well and received such high acclaim, they soon opened a restaurant right there on their property.

In its heyday Griffis Fish Camp hosted many cabins, male and female bath houses, screened fish-cleaning stations, a store, taxidermy services, and the small restaurant. The Griffis enterprise thrived for several decades until Lem, much older than his lovely bride, passed away in 1968, "just plain give out". Miss Alice, heartbroken, hung on and ran the fish camp for almost thirty years longer until she passed away in 1995. In later years, after they retired, sons Arden and Alpin joined her in the operation.

All the Griffis children attended college and became productive citizens, contributing generously to their local community and to society's greater good.

Alpin, with a Master's of Education, held the prestigious position of Clinch County school principal for decades. Arden, with an electrical engineering degree from Georgia Tech, worked for RCA and traveled the world. He returned to his family's homestead when he contracted cancer, likely caused by the radiation he received working on radar installations. Maldine served as a nurse in the hospital in Homerville, just up the highway a bit. Mary Alice, the youngest, a child prodigy on piano, was, from the age of three, able to play by ear classical music she heard on the radio.

Miss Alice blamed herself for not allowing Mary Alice the professional training and the creative outlets she needed. Given the opportunity to send her to Juilliard at a young age, Miss Alice declined. She reasoned that Mary Alice, too young and too naïve, would not survive being away from her secluded home on the banks of the Suwannee River. So Mary Alice played, not on the world stage, but instead on local school and church stages.

She remained in the quiet life of rural Georgia until college. In her third quarter at the University of Georgia she succumbed to a nervous breakdown and never recovered. Like her older brother Arden, she returned to the comfort of Griffis Fish Camp to live alongside her mother. Mary Alice died only a few months after her dearly beloved mother.

On our way to Mixon's Hammock we stopped to admire the alligators sunning on the logs. They looked surreal, draped luxuriantly across logs at the water's edge. Soaking up the last warming rays of

Gator Mirror

sunshine for the day, reluctant to give up their warm spots, they allowed us to approach, all 15 noisy canoes of us.

As an added enrichment to the experience, I taught my charges to yelp like baby alligators. I explained that even though momma and daddy alligators don't feed their young, they do offer protection from animals that might find the babies tasty. All they need do is yelp. If an adult, any adult, hears that yelp, a reptilian cry of distress, the call is answered. The perpetrator is summarily addressed with the adult gators attempting to dispatch the animal trying to eat the hatchlings.

As it turned out, my young charges had just the right frequency in their voices to perfectly imitate young alligators in distress. Their little high pitched yelps sounded very much like the "nyuck, nyuck, nyuck" that Curly Howard of the Three Stooges uttered in short-lived triumphant moments. To adult alligators my little canoeists sounded like their own offspring. Wow! Who knew?

Baby gators will even yelp inside their eggs when ready to hatch. Many an attentive, devoted mother alligator has been observed digging into the nest she has been dutifully protecting from late May to early August to free her young from the earthy confines of their compost-like womb. On rare occasions she has been observed transporting the hatchlings in her mouth from nest to water. The vegetation mom scrapes into a pile with her body actually incubates the eggs to the right temperature. As the vegetation decomposes it gives off heat just right for incubating her eggs.

Mom's attentiveness is one of several characteristics zoologists attribute to their closeness to birds. Avian mothers tend a nest to give warmth and protection. Since crocodilians (alligators, crocodiles, gavials, and caimans) are ectothermic (aka poikilothermic, or cold-blooded), they are incapable of incubating their own eggs. So they let the decomposing vegetation piled up into a nest provide warmth while they dutifully guard it from marauding skunks, raccoons, opossums,

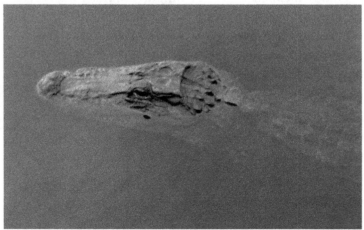

Head of an 8' Gator

snakes, turtles, herons, egrets, etc. who find their leathery, viscous eggs tasty.

Another characteristic that closely links crocodilians to birds is that they have a four-chambered heart, just like us mammals do. All other reptiles have three-chambered hearts. Evolutionary slides and crossovers from one phylum or class to another is really quite interesting to study.

Another stunning discovery is that the temperature of the nest determines sex.

If the nest temperature is 92°F and higher, males are produced. If the temperature averages 86°F and lower, females are produced. Within a nest temperatures can vary, and therefore so do the sexes of the hatchlings.

In nature, natural selection favors production of females. It makes sense. One male can impregnate many females.

In sea turtles just the opposite happens. Nest temperatures of 92°F and higher produce females, and temperatures 86°F and lower produce males. Temperatures in between produce a mixed nest.

This makes sense too. A sea turtle's nest on a hot white sand beach exposed to full sunlight will most likely reach temperatures at or above 92°F. An alligator's nest, on the other hand, will be cooler since they tend to construct their nests near cooling waters and most frequently in shade. The decomposing compost pile gives off heat, but it is low heat.

So one way to remember this interesting fact is: sea turtle females are hot, and alligator females are cool. Catchy, yes?

My young third graders yelped. All of them. To my surprise adult alligator heads popped up everywhere, answering my reptilian-humanoid charges' calls for help. Our canoes, however, defused the situation. Even an alligator is intimidated by something larger than itself. Fortunately a canoe is.

We arrived at Mixon's and took the way-too-many trips from landing area to campsite to unpack our canoes and set up camp. We looked like ants traveling from food source to nest. Some of the kids even said, "Bread and butter," as they passed each other along the long trail. I remembered that from a Warner Brothers cartoon when I was a kid. They must have made a new version of that ant cartoon.

Nowadays the campsite is right next to the canoe landing. On this trip though the campsite seemed miles away, located a quarter mile from the landing. Fortunately many hands make quick work. We had our big tent city set up in no time. The kids quickly collected downed tree limbs and branches for the campfire. S'mores are standard fare on kid camping trips and a campfire an absolute necessity.

"So, how do you want to divvy up the evening?" asked Martha. Ever the practical one, she needed to know the next steps.

"Let's see, Kimba, how 'bout you, Martha, Pedro, and Jock take charge of cooking dinner, and I'll do cleanup with Lori, Elise, and Rubin? Then we can move right into our evening activities."

"Done!" "Done!" "And done!" They all agreed to my suggestions. It's so nice when everyone is so agreeable.

Kimba, Martha, Pedro, and Jock oversaw the five kids assigned to help prepare dinner. One of the aspects of these trips is that everyone pitches in to do each part of the camping experience. Even though we didn't trust the kids to be left to their own devices in food preparation, especially around the stoves, we tried not to hover too much. If it looked like the food preparation edged towards burn mode, we quickly stepped in. Eating well is the key to happy campers. Burned food does not make a happy camper, and, strangely, it makes for very grumpy leaders.

While Lori, Elise, Rubin, and I helped the six kids assigned to clean-up, we chatted about the evening program.

"I really have this great ghost story I want to tell the kids. It'll just scare the pants off them," said Lori, obstinately dodging my objections.

"Yeah, Lori, I'm not a fan of ghost stories. I don't know your kids. You obviously do, and so you have the final say. I just really strongly urge you not to go there."

We discussed a short night paddle to shine alligator eyes and decided we could just ease our canoes out of the docking area to shine. Gators would be everywhere. We would see their eyes shining back rosy red all around us. But I had reservations.

Lori wanted to give her kids the full experience. So to allay my angst about taking such young kids on the water, she suggested we put several kids in each canoe with an adult in the stern. We would divide the kids into two groups with two adults left on shore to monitor those not canoeing.

Sounded like a reasonable plan.

We gathered our co-leaders to apprise them of our plan, and they all agreed it seemed reasonably safe and more importantly would surely be one of their most memorable life experiences.

Next we gathered up the kids and told them the plan for the next hour or so. They were giddy. Shining gator eyes! What fun! Ooo, how scary, on the water at night!

Kimba and I would be on the water with both groups, and Lori and Martha would be on the island with both

Barred Owl

groups. Jock, Elise, Pedro, and Rubin would paddle with us. What could go wrong?

I learned later that Lori hung back not out of altruism to let her co-workers have the experience, but because, as we paddled to Mixon's Hammock earlier that afternoon, she had had a bad flashback.

As a teenager on a summer family vacation, she swam out one afternoon to the middle of a lake by herself. Not a good idea, but she felt accomplished enough as a swimmer to do it. As she neared the floating platform in the middle of the lake, where she could rest and sunbathe, she saw something floating near it. She swam slowly towards the object and then froze. There in the water with her was a dead body. The unfortunate's back and head bobbed at the surface, and long hair rippled out with the motion of the waves.

She screamed and screamed and sucked up a lot of water. She barely made it to the platform. There she sat paralyzed all afternoon. Alone. The body bobbed up and down and at one point bumped against the platform when the wind picked up.

When she didn't show up for dinner, her parents worried. With his binoculars Lori's father spotted her on the platform, hugging her legs to her chest, rocking back and forth. Had she been like that all afternoon? He raced his boat to retrieve her. The local police pulled the body in later that same day.

I don't know how you get over experiencing something like that and I guess Lori still worked on it.

Before we left the campsite with the first group of kids, a pair of Barred Owls let loose with a wonderful string of monkey calls. They are actually pair-bonding calls that sound like monkeys whooping and hollering. "Who Cooks for You? Who Cook for Me?" is the standard descriptive phrase said with melodic inflections by birders to remember their call. Their pair bonding calls however are more along the lines of "Ah, Ah, Ah, Ah Ha, Ah Ha" and "OOOooooahhh."

The first time you hear them calling to each other you really think you have been dropped off in a tropical jungle in Honduras.

As the hooting continued, other Barred Owls drew in from near and far, and the chorus really got quite loud and humorous. The kids just loved it! All of us did.

The kids began hooting like the Barreds. But their high-pitched voices just could not do justice to the owl's low-pitched hoots. Their young high voices were much better suited to being alligator hatchlings.

Owls are wonderful birds of prey in general. Barred Owls are the most often heard birds in the Swamp. They hunt at night when other birds are tucked into their roosting positions for the dark hours. Owls' feathers are, well, feathered on the edges allowing them silent flight. In contrast, hawks' and eagles' feathers are straight edged. When they take flight, you hear whooshing sounds as their straight-edged feathers cut through the air.

Owls have large eyes that let in the slightest, dimmest light. Feathers around their eyes form saucers that help gather dim light as well. Even if no light is to be had, on the very darkest of dark nights, owls can still hunt successfully. Their ears are slightly offset on either side of their head. This allows them to pinpoint accurately where a mouse shuffles in the leaves as it forages or a frog trills in the night for a mate. I have had owls fly in to a branch over my head and not know it until they hooted right into my ear at head level. Now that is quite shocking!

Back in the late 1970's and early 1980's respectively, I had the great pleasure of helping raise a parent-less baby Screech Owl, Ollie, and caring for an impaired Great Horned Owl, Owlbert. For Ollie our biggest challenge was teaching him to hunt. We ended up pulling the back legs off crickets and grasshoppers for the first few times so he could get the hang of hunting. I felt badly about doing that but I didn't see another way to accomplish teaching a young owl to hunt considering my human limitations.

Owlbert looked fine in right profile. In left profile, he lacked an eye and wing courtesy of connecting with a car. Owlbert lost the bout. No matter. We got around his limitations by raising rats that were humanely euthanized in what seemed to us a pleasant gradual final slumber induced in a gas chamber of CO_2.

One afternoon while chatting to Owlbert he leaned forward on his perch, spread his impressive right wing to full length, opened his beak fully and to my great surprise and delight, upchucked a beautiful alabaster white rat pellet. Wow, I felt honored!

Moon Set at Cedar Hammock in Mizell Prairie

From that day forward, Owlbert regurgitated his pellet when I presented him with his daily ration of rat. His pellets became teaching tools at Oatland Island Education Center where I taught.

The first group loaded into the canoes with three kids to a canoe and one of us adults in the stern. We pushed off into the darkness. The kids all had their flashlight beams moving here and there, up and down from treetops to water and occasionally into our eyes. Not cool. Kimba shouted out that they needed to hold their flashlights to their foreheads and look down the beam for the red eyes.

Squeals of delight ensued as a child in this canoe, another over in that canoe, and yet another over there realized they were shining the eyes of alligators. What a moment! In just a few minutes they all caught on, and we jack-lit alligators everywhere. Dozens and dozens of rosy-red eyes surrounded us.

One of the girls began yelping like a baby gator. Then they all yelped. The chorus effectively brought out even more eyes.

Wider spaced eyes. Disturbingly wide.

"STOP. STOP. NO MORE YELPING!!!" Panicking a bit, I really didn't want alert, hyper-protective adult alligators converging on our distressed-hatchling-mimicking young human ones.

Pedro, who had read a bit but not quite enough on alligators said, "Miss Cathy, they eat their young, don't they? Vámonos?"

"Well, you're partially correct," I said. "Alligators eat their young only in times of drought when there's no other food source available. Makes sense really. It takes tremendous energy to get a hatchling from egg to reproductive age. So it's a hard fact that it's better to sacrifice the young of one year, so the adult has that much greater potential to reproduce the very next year and the next and the next. To stay alive this year the adult must eat its own young. It happens rarely, only in extreme drought when no other food's available."

I turned my attention back to my little charges. "Okay, my little charming hatchlings, let's head back to the dock and the island!"

The kids did as instructed, and all canoes performed admirable 180's to return to Mixon's Hammock.

The second set of kids were very ready for their adventure. As they loaded, I heard one of the outgoing kids say to an incoming kid, "Watch out for Big Hand." Then the kid laughed ghoulishly, "Brooooaaaaaaaa, Broooooooaaaaaaaa!"

Yikes, had Lori told her ghost story in spite of my objections?

The second outing with the kids went pretty much the same as the first. The kids just couldn't help themselves and yelped nearly right from the start. Kimba yelled this time to spare my voice. It's nice to know what the other leader needs at any given moment. The alligators were still in place against the side of the banks under logs along the bases of the red maples and hollies. The stars were glorious overhead. The night fantastic!

After the second canoe party returned to the island, we finished up dinner by roasting marshmallows and smashing them into submission onto a half of a Hershey's chocolate bar sandwiched in between two graham cracker halves. Voila, s'mores! We had to remind the kids to blow on the marshmallows to extinguish any flames. Reflexively though they all wanted to whiffle their torches of flaming sugar through the air. I had seen this activity result in too many launches of hot burning sugary projectiles.

On only one awful occasion a flaming marshmallow landed on a kid's cheek. No good. "Blow, blow, blow," became the mantra.

We began the evening's program energetically to burn off the sugar and any last vestiges of energy.

Immature White Ibis

A game of Duck, Duck, Goose lasted way too many rounds with this large group. Then we limbered up our vocal chords to sing a few camp songs that everyone knew; most I didn't, but they all did. We played campfire games with lots of hand slapping hand, hand slapping thighs, hand slapping the next person's thigh, hand thumping chest, etc. I didn't know those either.

Finally we settled our little campers down to review the day's and night's activities. We talked about the Barred Owls, herons, egrets, vultures, turtles, and of course the alligators. Lots of questions were asked and answered. These were sharp kids to a one.

Just before we released them to settle into their sleeping bags for the night, I admonished them to remove all food items from their tents since we were in Raccoon and Black Bear territory. None of us wanted to have to shoo away a Raccoon or, heaven forbid, fight a Black Bear over a piece of gum in the middle of the night. An amazing pile accumulated as the kids removed their stashes from their tents. We dutifully placed all the food items in our bear-proof and raccoon-proof boxes. At least, we hoped they would prove to be so this night.

With all the kids in their tents the adults lingered by the warmth of the flickering campfire a bit longer. One of us would spread the logs and douse the fire before we retired. For now though, the fire felt warm and inviting to just sit by and chat adult to adult. We kept our voices low so the kids wouldn't want to get back up to join us. But we really laughed quite a bit, especially about how well the kids could imitate the yelping of baby alligators and how all those widely spaced rosy-red eyes popped up everywhere.

I had just opened my mouth to ask Lori how she had entertained the kids while we were gone when a blood-curdling scream tore through the chilly night air.

"AAAAAAAAARRRRRRRRREEEEEEEEEEEEEEEEE"

Egad! We all leapt to our feet. Hearts pounded. Stomachs leapt into throats.

It took even me just a moment to understand the source.

No matter the source.

Immediately from all the tents in the huge semicircle around us came, "Big Hand! It's Big Hand! AAAAYYYYY-EEEE! Momma! Momma! Momma!"

I have never heard such a chorus of screams in so many different high-pitched little voices in my life.

My question as to how Lori had entertained the kids, loudly answered.

I gave her a withering look. Big Hand, really? She shrunk into her coat, pulling the collar up around her chin and ears.

The Barred Owl screamed again,

"AAAAAAAAARRRRRRRREEEEEEEEEEEEEEEE"

Then queried with its usual, "Who cooks for you? Who cooks for me?"

It didn't matter. From the entire tent city came another round of "Big Hand! It's Big Hand! AAAAYYYYYEEEE! Momma! Momma! Momma!"

Then the zippers unzipped. Twenty-two sleeping bag zippers and 22 tent zippers unzipped in short order, sounding quite like a chorus of wheezing cicadas.

By now all of us leaders were up and running towards the tents to comfort our frightened little campers.

Screaming, they poured out of their tents and were bee-lining it past us for the safety of the light of the campfire.

Big Hand would not come near the fire.

Really, Lori?

They huddled around the campfire hugging each other for comfort and then hugging an adult and then back to hugging each other and then several hugging one adult. We hugged a lot this night.

After a while I noticed they were all wet. Every slap one of them dripping wet. It took me a moment to figure out why.

I gave Lori another even more withering look.

"They're your kids. You're their mommy away from home. You get to deal with all these wet pajamas."

Lori groaned.

Pedro, Martha, Elise, Jock, and Rubin now joined me in giving Lori their most exasperated looks.

The kids were now gently held at arm's length to avoid further transfer of the wet stuff. We let them regroup to hug each other. They all were already wet anyway. So much for being consoling adults.

Kimba now directed her attention to Lori, "And you'll have to deal with all those wet sleeping bags too. You just might want to call in ole Big Hand to help you 'cause you're gonna need a real big helping hand with those 22 bags!"

And 22 tents. Twenty-two wet smelly tents.

I thought of the fragrant drive home in the van with all that pee-soaked gear. No good. What a pisser.

Too bad it hadn't "scared the pants off them."

Fragrant White Water Lily

CHAPTER 6

The New Mother

March 2013

Suzanna and I loaded our apple red 18' Indian River canoe to balance the weight just so for the most efficient paddling experience. Tom expertly loaded his yellow Necky kayak. Just before 10:00 AM we launched both into the Suwannee Canal. That's the deadline for launching set by the Okefenokee National Wildlife Refuge management. Their mandate is to manage for wildlife first, and for compatible use by humans second.

A few months earlier I had reserved the Purple Trail for our annual spring trip. The first night for Round Top platform and the second night at Coffee Bay. Coffee Bay originally built as a day-use platform served at this time as an overnight shelter as well. Intense lightening-ignited fires raged through large swaths of the Swamp from fall 2011 through late spring of 2012 destroying several overnight shelters.

Before launching I received a valuable warning from Chip Campbell. At that time, he and his wife Joy ran

Okefenokee Adventures, operated a store and café, and oversaw the boat ramp, boat rentals, and tours as the concessionaire for the refuge.

"Cathy, around MM2 in Grand Prairie, there's a new young mother gator who is just nuts. I'm not sure what she will do, but you just need to look out for her."

You pay attention to that kind of advice from a guy who is out there all the time. I thanked Chip for the heads-up and relayed the information to my paddling partners. Suzanna paid particular attention since she paddled in the bow of my canoe and would most likely be the first to connect with the nutty mother gator. Thomas sitting close to the water's surface in his nice sleek yellow Necky could go nose to nose with her. With Chip's words of caution still fresh, I feared Thomas' kayak might be a big yellow target. We loaded up and launched anyway.

Alligators are perhaps the most important megafauna we have in the southeastern USA for two reasons. First, just the movement of their bodies through waterways keep them open and unchoked with vegetation. Any paddler who has ever tried to work their way through a water hyacinth jam can thank our leathery friends for keeping those nuisance plants from filling in all of our waterways from bank-to-bank.

Water hyacinth is native to South America, but was introduced into the USA as an ornamental in 1884 at the Cotton States Exposition in New Orleans. Since then, it has had a life of its own as the bane of paddlers and at the expense of other native plants that it outcompetes. It is an invasive species that really thrives in its new found range.

The second reason alligators are so important is that they characteristically dig deep pools in front of their

Chip & Joy Campbell (Photo by Amy Thurman)

dens. This pool provides the gator refuge. Given a chance, a gator's first line of defense is to sink a foot or two below the water's surface. And, in times of drought, the gator holes will often be the only places where water remains. When the gator holes dry up, you know you are experiencing a severe drought.

The gator hole however is also the place many thirsty animals will make their way to for a drink. All the gator does is extract compensation every now and again with a random meal. Since an alligator doesn't eat every day, many more animals benefit than are consumed.

The Suwannee Canal is a straight shot for the first nine of the twelve miles to Round Top. When the weather is nice and there is little wind, the canal can be a bit boring. However on windy days (and there are many of those in the Swamp), I have been very thankful for the wind-breaks the tall cypress and stately pine trees lining the canal afford.

Digging of the Suwannee Canal began in September of 1891 with a private plan to drain the great Swamp for agricultural purposes. Peat is very fertile and would have supported abundant crops. Had the company succeeded in punching through Trail Ridge, the Okefenokee's eastern natural boundary, the Swamp would have drained into the St. Mary's River. And the mission of company president Colonel Henry Jackson would have been accomplished. The effort failed for many reasons, one of which was the death of poor Jackson after an appendectomy.

This day on the canal was lovely. We paddled several miles at a three-mile-an-hour pace. That's a perfect canoeing speed - no hurrying, no dawdling, just right and trust me, Suzanna, Thomas, and I have perfected the art of dawdling. When there is time to spare, we slow way down to take in every inch of the prairie or lake or canal. Today we weren't sure how much time we would need to address our mother gator, so we paddled at our normal pace.

Gators of varying sizes lined the canal with yellow-bellied sliders alongside in some places. These freshwater turtles coexist quite successfully side by side with alligators. Their shells are their main protection. One of the strongest structures in nature is the dome or the arch. After turtles reach a certain size, gators with their straight hard upper palates have a hard time

Chase Prairie on Purple Trail

crushing through the turtles' perfect defense of domed shells. The trick for turtles is to stay out of reach of those massive, albeit straight upper palate maws until they reach that magic shell size.

The wind was light, and we paddled on, knowing that Grand Prairie would be, well, majestically grand!

We ate a quick lunch at Coffee Bay standing up since we had been sitting for two hours as we paddled the first six miles. While munching wraps of hummus, lettuce, tomatoes and string cheese, and bacon for Thomas and me, we searched the open prairie behind Coffee Bay for Sandhill Cranes and herons and egrets. Even though none were spotted we still enjoyed the lovely vista of saw grass and lily pads and the emerging light green needles of the cypress trees. What a gorgeous view!

Then we took up our paddles and stroked rather quickly the next three miles to the turn into Grand Prairie.

"Ahhhh," we sighed collectively as we made that right turn into the Grand Prairie. Stretching out before our eyes as far as we could see the most glorious color palette of vibrant green, deep gold, rose red, alabaster white, pastel yellow, delicate lavender, and electric purple. Wow!!!

I stopped paddling and stood up to take it all in as a very wide smile spread across my face. I raised my arms upward, outstretched in a gesture of deep gratitude. This is my sanctuary. This is where I feel most reverent and most grateful.

The gold, red, and white flower spikes of golden clubs (also known as neverwets) pointed with me skyward. The blossoms of the fragrant white water lilies splayed open in full alabaster white glory with their large vibrant green Pac-Man-shaped pads newly formed. The light wind upended some of them, revealing the deep rose underneath, a result of an absence of chlorophyll on that side. No need to use up precious chlorophyll unnecessarily in places "where the sun don't shine".

Tiny pastel yellow and delicate lavender bladderwort flowers punctuated the dark water with their floating stem systems slightly submerged. Their tiny green bladders awaited triggering by even tinier aquatic insects.

The bladders implode when their hair-like triggers are touched. The triggering insect or crustacean is swept into the bladder by a difference in pressure, where the plant's digestive enzymes begin work immediately.

There are several insectivorous plants in the prairies – three different species of pitcher plants, one species of sundew and four species of bladderworts. Nutrients are not readily available due to the anaerobic condition of the substrate. The pH of the water is so acidic few decomposers, fungi and bacteria, can survive in it. So some plants have bypassed this small challenge by extracting nutrients from insects that have been dining on other successful nutrient-accessing plants. Clever system.

Blue Flag Iris (Iris virginica)

The sizzling blue purple of the blue flag iris
popped out spectacularly, electrifying the wet-scape
beautifully. Like Monet splashes on a canvas.

Suzanna took her turn standing up, reinvigorating her backside and attesting to the incredibly gorgeous prairie. In his kayak Thomas showed his appreciation by stretching only. He did not stand up, a much trickier action in that tippy vessel.

We paddled on through the magical landscape welcomed by a pair of trumpeting Florida Sandhill Cranes. A Great Blue Heron grumpily winged off past moss-draped cypress trees. Two Red-tailed Hawks screeched overhead spiraling upward in their gracefully choreographed aerial mating flight.

A view like this - all the color, all the life - takes your breath away. It is just that beautiful. This is why you paddle these many miles. This is your fantastic reward. This gorgeous Swamp is like no other place anywhere in the world. And it is right here in our back yard, in the southeastern corner of our great state of Georgia.

Suzanna put her paddle across her lap and just stared with a big pleased grin as I moved us forward. Thomas held back to enjoy an unobstructed view. He had been staring at our derrières the entire way. I suggested that he take the lead for a while, so that he could see without us blocking his view. But, with the specter of the impending encounter with the new mother gator on his mind, he graciously declined the offer.

We paddled on quietly past mile one. As we approached mile two, I stopped for a strategy planning session.

"So, Chip said the new mother gator would most likely be just past the big left turn past mile marker two, and I can see the mile marker up ahead."

Suzanna turned in her seat to better hear. Thomas pulled alongside. They both leaned in, listening intently.

"Thomas, as we approach the area where she is, please stay close behind us. And then, as we come alongside of her, pass us on the opposite side. Does that sound like a good plan of action?"

My paddling companions trusted my years of experience and now how to deal with this situation based on those years of experience. They both nodded in agreement.

Thomas hung back just a bit as Suzanna put full muscle into each stroke. We made a nice wake, and soon we passed Purple Trail MM2 in Grand Prairie.

Suzanna turned her head for me to hear. "You know I love being in the bow so I can see everything first, but I'm not so sure I want to be up here right now!" she chuckled nervously.

"Ah, piece of cake! We'll shoot past her before you and she can blink an eye."

Tom on Minnie's Lake

As we rounded the big left turn, Suzanna heard her hiss before seeing her. For a small thing momma gator had built up a lot of attitude and let us know right off the bat of her displeasure. Her hiss, the intensity of a punctured high-pressure tire, was impressively loud and forceful. She menacingly and effectively conveyed her intense irritation with our intrusion of her swampy idyll.

Suzanna and I stopped as planned to allow Thomas to pass us on the side opposite the hissing momma. Her small babies strung out all around her. They yelped loudly in their primordial throaty distress calls. Momma's eyes were hugely alert. She would not let anything hurt her babies nor pass through her territory it seemed.

In my more than 300 daylight and overnight trips into the Swamp, I experienced only a single, what I would call intense, encounter with an alligator. That with a blind ten-foot mother. I felt sympathy for her, but didn't appreciate her coming under my canoe to topple it. All she wanted was to move my canoe, the intruder, out of her territory. It worked. I left her territory. In a hurry.

This was about to be my second intense encounter.

And this mother could see. At only five feet long, a new mother to be sure.

Female alligators can mate as small as six feet when they are 10-15 years old. They continue to grow up to about ten feet in length as their maximum. Males on the other hand mature earlier at 8-12 years old. They really never reach a maximum size but rather just keep on growing until they die. Of course their growth rate slows considerably as they age. Like human males, they stop growing in length or height, adding girth instead.

The largest gator I have ever seen in the wild remains at 15 feet. Trust me, when you see one that size, you paddle carefully and cautiously. They are leftovers from the age of dinosaurs and have small brains. Their ancestors can be traced back 180 million years, and back then they were way bigger...and with small brains.

The canoe trail in Grand Prairie barely wide enough for our canoe would be a very tight squeeze for the kayak. Thomas paddled up to our starboard side and in a few paddle strokes unexpectedly and unintentionally ran up onto a peat blowup ever so slightly submerged and out of his line of sight. He stuck solidly.

Peat blowups are literally just that – peat blown up to the surface by gas. In the Okefenokee's acidic waters bacteria and fungi, the primary decomposers, do not thrive well. Some do manage, but because the rate of decomposition is so slow, thick layers of plant debris (peat) build up over time. Beneath that debris, the fungi and bacteria do their work, slowly but surely. Trapped pockets of methane, the byproduct of their labor, build up below the peat. Eventually that trapped methane blows chunks of peat, from inches to feet thick, up to the surface. This newly air-exposed or oxygenated peat now becomes very fertile soil. Seeds and spores landing there find nutrients galore, and growth begins immediately.

The word "Okefenokee" comes from the Creek language and means "land of trembling earth". I have taken many paddling guests for walks on this watery trampoline; it always transforms them into giggling children re-discovering a familiar phenomenon, like a mud puddle after a warm rain. It is always great fun, but not today, not right now. Thomas was royally stuck on it.

Momma gator ramped up her game. She lunged towards the rear of the canoe, right where I sat.

I stood up. A tall vertical profile is much more intimidating to a gator than a squat low profile.

She backed off, but only for a moment. Thomas struggled to extricate himself from his predicament.

Momma lunged again, coming a bit closer than her previous effort. More aggressive this time, she aimed higher up on the side of the canoe. My heart pounded, and my stomach churned.

Momma lunged again, a bit higher, almost to my shin. I yelled, "Thomas, now!"

With a mighty push, Thomas moved off the peat blowup. Now he had the difficult task of choosing an alternate route still on the starboard side. There weren't many choices except one, scraping sides with us.

Momma lunged again and hit the side of the canoe with a loud thwack, knocking me down to a sitting position.

Suzanna turned to see what had happened and rocked the canoe to port. I grabbed the gunnel to keep us

12' Gator

upright, and my paddle dropped to the bottom of the canoe. I reached down to grab it just as momma hit a bit higher on the side of the canoe.

I stood up again and used my treasured ash bent shaft paddle to fend her off. That paddle was a work of art, a present from a longtime friend. Momma could have made toothpicks out of it in short order. Too distraught to think clearly, I did not exchange it for my extra aluminum-shafted plastic-bladed cheaper paddle instead.

I yelled at Suzanna, "Stabilize the canoe with your paddle!" And she did immediately. I yelled at Thomas, "Get going, she's not happy, and neither am I!"

He earnestly tried but not hard enough for me. Momma lunged again, higher than before, and knocked me to my seat again.

Thomas, thankfully, just in the nick of time, navigated a new course to squeeze past us. I yelled to Suzanna, "Paddle, paddle like hell!" And she did.

Momma lunged one more time, snapping as she came over the gunnel and this time missing my left thigh by a mere inch.

My heart leapt into my throat, and a rush of adrenaline took control. I dug my paddle into the peat right beside her small head with her fiercely blazing eyes. I dug so hard the canoe rocketed forward.

Suzanna nearly catapulted out of the bow. She responded in kind and also dug hard as we zoomed away without looking back.

Thomas already neared the platform. Intent on getting out of our way and away from momma, he hadn't stuck around for the show.

I shook the entire rest of the short way to Round Top. I literally shook. That was only the second time I have shaken from fright in the Swamp. The first was that large momma who tried to tip over my canoe.

There up ahead Round Top's utilitarian chemical toilet silhouetted out of place against the gorgeous backdrop of the broad expanse of Grand Prairie. It is not generally pleasing to the eye. But today it welcomed us, guiding us to the much needed shelter of that good platform.

Upon reaching the approximately 20' by 30' wooden platform, our fortress from the ravages of battle, we all sprawled out in sheer relief. I think I actually nodded off for a few moments.

Thomas, first to break the reverie of our much needed down time, droned in his deep soft drawl, "Well, that was exciting. I didn't know if I was going to get off that blowup in time or not. Thank you for so kindly running interference."

Suzanna responded in her more rapid Bostonian accent, "Unbelievable! I wasn't at the business end, but from up front, that was really intense."

"Yep, intense," I agreed from under my hat that shielded the lowering sun.

We spent all that evening recounting every detail of what I think had actually occurred in only a minute of adrenaline rush. At the time it seemed an eternity.

As the last drops of pinot noir dripped from the second bottle of our evening's allotment into our stainless steel stemware, I had an unnerving thought.

We were going to pass by her again on our way out the next morning, and she would no doubt be ready for us. Her small brain focused on defending her brood, her territory. Great, just great.

I didn't say as much to my beloved companions. The last few minutes of our long day's paddle had really drained us, and I wanted them to sleep safe and secure like well cared for babies. Of course, they too had come to the same conclusion and slept more like babies awaiting the sharp stab of a needle in a pediatrician's office.

Dawn washed over the Swamp with rays of sunshine kissing our three tents pitched perfectly on our little platform. First things first; my coffee drinkers were in need of their morning cup of Joe.

I civilly sipped my morning ration of green tea while I prepared a hearty breakfast of eggs sautéed into caramelized onions and wilted spinach atop dinner leftovers.

"So," Thomas began, "I am the most vulnerable in my Necky, and I know we go right past our nemesis again this morning. What's the plan, oh great and wise Swamp Goddess?"

My companions knew how I got my nickname. They had heard all the stories over the many years we had been coming into this most hallowed of places.

"Glad you ask. I've been thinking about this all night, and the only good solution I've come up with is to put

Suzanna Setting Up Camp at Round Top

you in the middle of our canoe and tow your kayak.
I'm afraid momma is going to be ready for us, and
she'll go after the lowest profile, and that will be you
in your lovely shiny yellow Necky."

"I agree," Thomas drawled softly, nodding. "I don't
want to be her main target today, and I promise I'll
paddle as instructed without objection."

"So we put some of the things that are now in the
middle of our canoe in his kayak? Is that the plan?"
Suzanna reasoned.

"Yep, that'll work," I agreed.

We finished up breakfast, took down our tents, and
stuffed our respective gear and clothing bags. I got in
the canoe while Thomas and Suzanna dutifully pulled
the gear bags to the edge of the platform for me to
pack just so. Things that were to go in the kayak were
directed there. In short order we were ready to paddle.

Each of us "powdered our noses" one more time, to

145

lighten the load, so to speak.

With Thomas in the middle, taking up one of the spare paddles, we pushed off from the incredibly picturesque panoramic view of my favorite campsite in the entire Swamp, Round Top. Many memorable events have happened here or on the way to it, and on this trip we had already added one more big memory.

"Suzanna, you'll most likely see her first, so let us know when you do. On my order, we paddle like hell." I sounded confidently in charge of the situation.

"I'm on it," she vowed.

"I'm good here," added Thomas.

Thomas, a bit unsteady in his middle position, since it was higher than his seat in the kayak, admirably held his own while wielding an aluminum straight-shafted single-bladed plastic paddle. The one I should have grabbed to stave off momma the day before instead of my treasured bent shaft ash paddle.

His sleek yellow Necky trailed behind us. It added only a bit of drag, but, with a gator ahead, it felt like a sea anchor slowing us considerably. In my mind, this alternative far, far safer.

We paddled about twenty canoe-lengths when Suzanna stiffened, "There she is!"

"Paddle, paddle hard like your life depends on it," I yelled, "because it does!" And we did.

We shot past the new mother, her fierce eyes blazing, laser-focused on the canoe.

She lunged as we came abreast of her, hitting the canoe just behind Thomas and in front of me.

We all jumped but maintained balance and good paddling form. We paddled more in earnest now. The attack had begun.

She recoiled and lunged again in time to hit the stern just behind me.

We paddled harder, grunting with every stroke. We were a well-oiled machine.

I am positive we could have out stroked a Harvard rowboat team. We paddled intently, in unison. We had only one goal. Get past momma.

I looked back in time to see momma make one last mighty lunge in renewed effort and even greater determination than before.

"Oh, My God," I yelled. "Dig hard, dig hard."

And Thomas and Suzanna did. Both in their mid-70's they were in amazingly good shape.

We didn't let up until we reached Purple Trail MM2 in Grand Prairie. There we rested and shifted everything back to original positions. Carefully moving gear out of

Healthy Gator

147

the kayak cockpit, replacing it with Thomas.

We paddled the last mile through Grand Prairie in the silence of profound reverence and utter thankfulness. How can you not be grateful in such splendid natural grandeur?

Upon reaching our overnight stop an hour and a half later down the famous Suwannee Canal at Coffee Bay platform, we unloaded our gear and set up camp.

The rest of that afternoon we explored Chase Prairie behind our campsite on the southern side of the Suwannee Canal. Sandhill Cranes, a few Snowy and Great Egrets, and a large group of White Ibises dotted the vast green and gold grassy wetland. We appreciated completely relaxing. The attack of our nemesis with her snapping leathery jaws armed with conical sharp white teeth had been unnerving.

That evening we sipped our ration of pinot noir and made dinner while recounting the day's activities. Of course our successful navigation past, and escape from, our aggressive new mother the hot topic.

In her defense, we all understood her actions and took no offense at them. New mothers are always the most protective of their offspring. Human mothers are too, even though ferocity in most tapers off with second and third children. I know. I am a second child.

Suzanna loved her vegetables warm but crisp; surprisingly Thomas, a southerner through and through, also leaned toward the al dente prep. They decided to cook the greens left in our cooler. I watched as they sprinkled in spices and sautéed them in olive oil. I knew their quick preparation would not be suitable for me. I like my greens slowly cooked all day long with ham hocks or ribs for seasoning. My preparation preference likewise would not have gotten past Suzanna's lips, our vegetarian New Englander.

Coffee Bay Platform

When they deemed the greens edible, they dug in and raved at how delicious they were. I knew better, but I politely let them coax me into trying a forkful. I curled my lips and slipped the greens in quickly. And just as quickly they involuntarily spewed back out. I just couldn't. They weren't right.

I regained my composure, apologized profusely, cleaned up my green spew and thanked them for trying, but they were a no go for me. Even some good hot-pepper vinegar would not have made them edible. Warm raw greens, yuck!

I steered the conversation back to our brush with momma. "So, I thank you both for following my instructions and urgent barks when the occasion arose. You all are the best!"

My appreciation was sincere. I really enjoyed spending time with both Suzanna and Thomas in the Swamp, in the Everglades, on barrier islands, anywhere.

Suzanna, a retired physical therapist from Boston, had

become my dear friend after years of paying to come on my trips. I visit her in winter for snow-shoeing. She keeps in terrific shape by walking, lifting weights, and practicing Tai Chi. She is a wonderful mother to her son and daughter-in-law and a fabulous grandmother.

Thomas, a retired thoracic surgeon, and beloved uncle of my dear friend Kim, hails from Thompson, Georgia, and now Aiken, South Carolina. He is the quintessential southern gentleman and a wonderful family man. He paddles quite a bit with other friends who live closer by and always reads up on the human history of any place we visit before we go there, so we always benefit from his preparation.

I love them both. We have grown close over our many years of sharing excursions into the Swamp and other wild places.

"Now, I must tell you what really happened as we passed our mother gator."

"Oh, we thought we had heard it all." They looked at each other and then back at me. I had their undivided attention.

"Not quite all. The rest of the story is, as we passed momma I looked back after she hit the canoe the second time just behind me. I wanted to see if the kayak tether needed to be untied. Momma made one more lunge, and this time she went right over the cockpit of your kayak, Thomas!" I gestured an exaggerated arc trajectory with my arm to illustrate her coming out of the water and over Thomas' kayak.

It was their turn to spew.

They both bent forward reflexively. This night's precious allotment of pinot noir sprayed involuntarily from their mouths in long impressive reddish purple arches. I automatically jumped back to avoid the shower.

Suzanna, Tom & Cathy at Minnie's Lake Shelter

"What?! Oh My God!!! Are you kidding me?!" They both choked and coughed and sputtered in utter disbelief.

They looked at each other and then at me, shaking their heads. Now embarrassed at the aftermath of their response to my revelation, they wiped their mouths and then dutifully mopped up red spew from the table, bench and deck. Eventually they regained composure.

Thomas then rumbled as he laughed. "I wondered why the cockpit felt so wet when I got back into it!"

E pilog:

In all the hundreds of trips I have made through the Swamp, and through all of the thousands of pleasant, respectful encounters I have had with alligators, only two have been intense. Those two intense moments involved mothers protecting their young and I have no problem with that. I figured out long ago how to work around them and enjoy the Swamp alongside them. It has been a good relationship through all of these decades.

Issues arise when encountering mothers of any species while protecting their young. They will risk their own safety and well-being to protect their young and alligators are no exception. Problems also happen when humans, most likely in an effort to gain a better view, block off escape routes. I have seen this time and time again. A photographer anxious to get a close up hangs over the side of their boat within inches of the snout of a gator. I always scream for them to get back. Geesh, what were they thinking?

The other issue is when humans feed wild animals and the animals then associate humans with food. When the next human encountering the same wild animal does not know of previous humans' feeding activities, a negative encounter ensues. The animal now expects all humans to feed them and when food is not produced the animal can become aggressive.

Chillin' Gator Style

Also in the case of large alligators especially, a human swimming, typically in a horizontal orientation, can become food for a big gator. In Florida particularly in the central Florida Springs area around Ocala, signs are posted in certain areas known to be inhabited by large alligators. It is very wise to heed those signs that state "No Swimming, Alligators Present". Alligators size up prey by length on the horizontal plane. To avoid an alligator attack, should you ever find yourself in such a situation, make yourself as vertical as possible.

In one encounter I heard about on Ossabaw Island, a Georgia Department of Natural Resources biologist, while leading a troop of Boy Scouts around the island, stooped to point out aquatic vegetation at the edge of a pond. The man stood over six feet tall and presented quite an obstacle to the unseen alligator submerged near the pond's edge in wait of drinking prey. When the biologist stooped down, changing his vertical profile to a much more manageable size according to the gator's perception, the gator took opportunity and lunged at the outstretched arm with pointing hand. The gator's mouth went half way up the unfortunate and very surprised man's arm. Of course the boys, horrified, screamed and moved back quickly. The

Gator at Billy's Lake South End Slough

biologist now with the alligator half way up his arm, took a few moments to figure out how to get the darn leathery animal off his arm. The only way to do this without doing more damage to his arm and the alligator was to drop back down to the ground to support the weight of the alligator's body. When that happened the alligator apparently realized the error and released the arm and backed into the water to await more suitable prey.

In any body of water in the southeast there will be an alligator inhabiting it or at least passing through at some point. I swim in most places, except where large alligators are known to be and certainly where signs are posted stating such. Alligators are naturally afraid of humans and especially where humans have shot at them or thrown sticks, bricks or other objects at them. Alligators may have small brains, but they have successfully survived and thrived for millions of years. Their instincts serve them well. They will shy away from bullets, bricks, sticks, etc. and those launching those harmful projectiles.

With a depressed economy in the south in the 1950's and concomitantly, with high demand for leathery alligator hides, American alligators nearly became extinct.

Poaching alligators for hides became big business in the southeast. In a few good nights of poaching, a good alligator hunter could make enough money to support his family for the entire year. It wasn't until the state of New York banned the importation of alligator hides that the economic basis for the business ended and therefore the poaching. To this day alligators, although they have recovered in numbers, are still listed as endangered due to their close resemblance to the really endangered American crocodile. Alligators can be legally taken by those with proper licenses and permits. Permitted alligator farms in south Georgia and north central Florida export meat and hides to foreign and domestic markets. In souvenir shops throughout the southeast you will find small preserved alligator heads.

Alligators are opportunistic feeders and will literally feed on anything that moves. Their individual size dictates what they can successfully swallow whole or take under water to drown. Smaller gators eat small things that move – frogs, insects, small fish, etc. Larger gators eat snakes, turtles, mammals and birds. Other naturalists state they have observed larger alligators pull deer underwater. Gators pull larger prey underwater when they come to the water's edge to drink. Carcasses are then stuffed up under submerged logs for tenderizing. Alligators cannot tear off chunks of meat successfully until the meat has been tenderized over several days underwater through the process of decay. When the meat is of sufficient condition, the alligator will latch on and then tear off a chunk by twisting its entire body lengthwise as if on a spit.

On one occasion I observed a gator at Suwannee Canal Recreation Area "playing" with a dead otter. I guessed the unfortunate otter wasn't paying attention or was otherwise compromised somehow to become prey. Typically otters do not come into the deep water when alligators are active. They stay up in the prairie areas to raise their kits while surviving off smaller fish, frogs and crustaceans. When temperatures turn cold late November through mid-March the gators don't eat and the otters then venture into the lakes and deeper channels for larger fish.

Alligators are ectothermic (or cold blooded) meaning their body temperatures are dependent on external temperatures. When they are cold, their metabolic rate slows down and they literally cannot manage digestion. Food will rot in their stomachs. So if you are afraid of being eaten by an alligator and want to see the Swamp, just come during the winter months when alligators are not eating.

On another occasion while serving as an interpretive naturalist on a birding excursion on a pontoon boat in the Altamaha River Delta, I, and everyone else on board that pontoon that particular trip, observed a +12' gator with a large black hog in its mouth. The very impressive wake created as the gator pushed his large prey down the river attracted our collective attention. It wasn't until our Captain Phillip Kempton steered close enough that we could see with binoculars the exact situation. That is the first and only time I have ever seen a gator with a hog.

On Little St. Simons Island in the early 1980's I observed a ten foot gator swimming with a six footer in his/her mouth. I guessed that situation to be a territorial dispute with the younger, smaller gator making a tactical error in trying to establish a denning site in or too close to the older, larger gator's territory.

There is a plethora of information on the natural history of alligators, so if you are interested, get going on the web!

Moon Reflection at Coffee Bay Platform

CHAPTER 7

Going Native

Maul Hammock

Fall 1997

"Uh, Miss Cathy, can we talk to you?"

"Sure, of course you may. What's up, gentlemen?"

"Well, ya see, Miss Cathy, Marcus and I don't, won't, er, just can't go into the Swamp with you. We've talked about it a lot, and we just don't want to do it."

"Okay, so tell me, gentlemen, what's the big problem?"

"Er, well, Miss Cathy, you know, we just don't think we can handle the whole Swamp deal. You know, things are different in there, really different."

"Ah ha, I get it, things are different in there, but that's the cool part. You're going to experience something 99% of folks on this good planet will never experience. And that would be a real shame if you pass on it now that you have the chance. So, just for grins, if you don't go, what'll you and Marcus do while the rest of us are in the Swamp?"

"Yeah, Miss Cathy, we already figured that one out, we'll just get a hotel room and wait for ya."

"Right, well, no, that won't work, gentlemen. You'd have to have a chaperon, and none of us adults are going to stay behind with you two. Have you spoken with Ms. Rabinski and Mr. Jones about this?"

"Nope, they wouldn't let us do this unless you agreed to it, so that's why we're coming to you first."

"Ah ha, I see. Well, did ya think I would really let you miss the Swamp?"

"Well. No. Maybe. But Miss Cathy, we really feel very strongly about this. We just can't, no, we won't go. That's it. We're not going in!"

Both boys crossed their arms in childish defiance. I waited for a bottom lip to protrude to complete the look. Josh complied. A very practiced pout to be sure.

"Okay, I understand. But what is it, exactly, that has you so dead set against going into the Swamp? Is it the alligators? Are you afraid snakes will drop out of the bushes into your canoe?"

"Well, Miss Cathy, those are all very scary, for sure, but you explained those, so I think we're good on those."

"All righty then, Josh, what exactly is the problem?"

"Well, uh, Miss Cathy, it's spiders. Black widow spiders to be exact."

"Really? That's it? Black widow spiders? Wow! Well, I didn't see that one coming! Gentlemen, I can tell you this. I've only seen a handful of them in the wild. Personally I think they're gorgeous spiders. And I've actually heard them before I've seen them. You can hear their hard shells tap on logs as they cross them. It's really quite cool."

"Yes, ma'am, we remember you saying that. But, but, what about the chemical toilets? What happens if we sit down on the seat, you know, to do our business, and, and, and one sneaks up from down below and bites us on the ass?"

I didn't see that coming either. I worked hard not to laugh out loud but couldn't help but smile. The imagery they conjured up was priceless. Their big fear focused squarely on getting bitten on the rear end during their most vulnerable moment. Geesh, this was a new one on me!

These teenagers, all boys, all ill-suited for the strictures of regular high school classrooms, had been sent away by their parents to a boarding school designed to help them develop social skills and prepare academically for college. Some came from old money families – Vanderbilt, Randolph, Morgan. Some of their surnames belied new wealth – Horowitz, Funderburk, Zhang. In

Big Water Run after Fire

most cases though, I think the parents sent their sons away for someone else to do the work they should have been doing themselves.

I didn't reprimand Josh for using the word "ass." I knew what battles to pick with teenagers. The battle being waged at the moment didn't hinge on word choice.

"Well, gentlemen, I've been sitting on those toilet seats for many decades, not that I particularly like it, and I've never ever been bitten by a spider, much less even seen a black widow in one of those essential privies. I can safely say, there's less than a tenth of one percent chance you'll be bitten by a black widow. On your ass."

"Yeah, well, okay thanks, Miss Cathy, but Marcus and I are firm about this. We just aren't going into the Swamp and that's that!"

I conferred with the school counselors. With Leah, Miss Rabinski, petite, blond, late twenties, already a well-seasoned counselor, especially well-versed in the shenanigans of teenage boys. And with Nathan, Mr. Jones, tall, skinny, dark shaggy beard, still learning the ropes. As I had figured, Marcus and Josh would be going into the Swamp. Leah and Nathan were dead set against calling the boys' parents to arrange for transport home or back to the school. The boys would just have to, as they said, "suck it up."

Okay then. Suck it up they would. Bottom lips back in, please. However, a situation like this can go a lot of different ways. I just didn't know which way this particular one would end up.

The boys' ultimatums had come after we had been hunkered down on Little Tybee Island for a day longer than scheduled because of a cold front that blew through unexpectedly hard. The 45-knot winds churned up the surf on the Atlantic side and kicked up high rollers in the creeks behind the island, making it too dangerous for us to paddle back to Tybee Island on the appointed day. So with lots of time to ruminate about the next part of our adventure, Josh and Marcus had worked their imaginations up into frenzied angst.

From many past trip experiences, I knew how to fill otherwise idle time. I pulled out group games and challenges to occupy the boys.

For this trip I started out with an active game of Predator-Prey. We had plenty of beach and lots of sand for drawing lines. I split the boys into two equal groups and had them stand shoulder to shoulder with their team mates facing the other group across a five foot swath of sand. Twenty feet behind each team was their goal, another line drawn in the sand. The hitch to the game is they cannot run. They can only hop on one foot. It is quite a comical sight and very challenging.

I call out a predator and a prey as I point to a side. For example as I point to one side I say grouper and as I point to the other side I say hammerhead shark. The boys have to decide if they are being eaten or doing the eating. If they are being eaten, they hop towards their goal. If they are tapped or eaten by a shark before reaching their goal, they simply change sides to become a shark. The shark eats the grouper and therefore the grouper now becomes a shark.

The really fun one is when I say human-mosquito. That one always confuses the heck out of them.

When they tire of Predator-Prey I go to a quieter game of balance. I don't remember the exact name of the game but it goes like this.

Two people of any size and any age face each other with elbows bent and palms close but not touching. Feet are apart just outside the hips with knees bent. The object of the game is to knock each other off

Female Anhinga Drying Wings

balance. I have seen very small kids win against really big kids. Usually the little kids figure out to use the bigger kid's bulk against him. As the big kid leans into trying to push hard on the smaller kid's palms, the smaller kid simply doesn't resist and the bigger kid topples over from his own unstoppable momentum thereby losing the round. The best two out of three rounds win the match.

They loved doing those two activities and a few more I pulled out. When I exhausted my repertoire, I challenged them to make up their own. They did fairly well until the challenges grew too rambunctious and I feared for their safety.

At that point I challenged them to something more benign – an impromptu talent show during which I wiggled my ears. Seeing an adult, their leader, wiggle her ears, elevated me to star status. My long dangling earrings emphasized the movement of my twitching lobes. My audience delighted in my newly revealed talent. But my poor head muscles ached later that

Maul Hammock Lake

night from being asked to reprise my talent again and again. They wanted to learn how to do it too. Who knew ear wiggling would be such a big hit? You know, Little Tybee's Got Talent!

Right after the Talent Show ended, thinking ahead to the Okefenokee, I taught them how to Swamp Holler. I explained that in the Okefenokee long before electronics were on the scene the only way to communicate long distances was by perfecting your hollering. If done well, a husband for instance could inform his wife miles out what he was bringing home for supper. More importantly Swamp Hollers were specific to the individual and allowed you to determine if friend or foe approached. For the most part though the old timers followed the "shoot first and ask questions later" protocol.

I demonstrated my own Swamp Holler that began on low notes at low speed crescendoing to high notes and high speed and ending in a very loud staccato of Ha, Ha, Ha descending notes. Sort of like this – yee......
yee......yee....Yee... YEE..YEE..HA..HA..HA..Ha....Ha....

ha....ha.

The boys went nuts. They loved it! They practiced doing their own long into the night. I heard them laughing at each other's and making comments as to the other's sounding like a wounded tomcat, a bellowing bull or a lovesick elk.

We explored every inch of Little Tybee and amassed an amazing shell collection for identification and discussion and later for a stacking game. The shell stacking game consists of players stacking their selected shells one after the other. The person that places the shell that topples the stack is the loser of that round and gets a point. At the end of the previously decided time period, the person with the lowest number of points wins. Too bad I didn't get a patent on this game concept. But then I am sure this game has been played for millennia with whatever objects happen to be on hand. Guale Indians probably played it when they had time to kill. Today of course a different twist on the concept is Jenga, which I adore. Jenga's beauty and brilliance is that it can be played with any number of players of any age, just like my stacking game.

Even with all these activities, the boys still had time on their hands to worry about our next adventure. Oh well. We were going into the Swamp, period. All of us, period. Together, period. The leaders had spoken.

The next day the wind subsided enough for us to pack up our now very sandy tents and gritty gear after digging out our kayaks that had become temporary sand dunes. We paddled the long way around the backside of Little Tybee Island to stay in the lee as much as possible. The shorter route around the front side was still too dangerous with the surf kicked up. We landed on Tybee three hours later, a bit longer than anticipated due to an unexpected delay.

Even though we paddled in the sheltered creeks behind the islands, one kayak had still managed to flip. Josh. Great. The only one to do so. I feared this mishap would only add more fuel to Josh's steadfast determination of not wanting to go into the "spider-infested" Okefenokee.

As soon as we made landfall we whisked Josh off to the motel to dry off and change clothes. The rest of the group helped load the kayaks onto the trailer and the gear into the van.

That night Leah and Nathan pow-wowed with the boys and laid down some hard-and-fast rules. Josh and Marcus would be going to the Swamp with everyone in their group, and they would all enjoy the experience. At the very least, no negative comments nor commentary would be allowed.

Kevin (my co-leader, really a trainee, medium build, long hair, neatly trimmed beard, early twenties, from Ohio) and I went to our homes to dry out and repack for the next day's journey to the Okefenokee. Our down day buffer between the two legs of this school's trip had been used up with our unexpected extended stay on Little Tybee Island. No matter. The food for the Swamp portion had already been bought and packed. We just needed to remember to get items out of the freezer and into the coolers before we left our headquarters. As part of Kevin's training, he assumed responsibility for the gear. I took charge of the food.

The next morning began way too early. We had to leave Savannah at 6:30 AM to make it to Suwannee Canal Recreation Area by 9:00 to catch the shuttle up to Kingfisher Landing to launch on the Red Trail. The boys looked fresh and ready to go. All except Josh and Marcus. They wouldn't look me in the eyes. I guessed they felt betrayed. I know parents get these looks all the time. That is what parenting

166

is all about. Setting limits, establishing boundaries, and delivering consequences when those limits and boundaries are breached. Yes, I parented quite a lot on these trips. Even when my "children" were decades older than me.

The funniest "parenting" or "refereeing" I do involves married couples. Often a husband wants to go on an adventure, and the wife dutifully goes along. On those occasions when neither has paddled before, I make an announcement at the beginning of the trip. It goes something like this, "I reserve the right to save marriages and maintain friendships by separating partners if need be." They laugh, but I am serious. I make the rules and in doing so I have saved many a marriage and even more friendships.

Most of the time the husband, larger, heavier, rightfully takes the stern, to trim the canoe and balance the load. His wife, typically lighter, smaller, occupies the bow. Steering is accomplished by the stern paddler with some help from the bow paddler in tight turns. If the canoe begins to follow a woefully inefficient zigzag course, the blame is often laid on the wife, in the bow, who is not the principal steerer, by the frustrated husband, in the stern, who is supposed to be the steerer.

Anyway, when I give my usual speech regarding "reserving the right", everyone gets it and accepts my authority.

Kevin, my co-leader, a clever young man, quite humorous, a history major, would go on to earn his Ph.D. in history and teach at the University of Georgia in Athens. I adored Kevin. Full of energy and funny stories already at his young age. Kevin's gear preparation for this trip included packing the kayaks for the island leg and the canoes for the Swamp leg. The one detail that slipped by him though – a big detail – was that

Water Spider Orchid (*Habenaria repens*) (Photo by Geoff Bulpitt)

there were an odd number of people in our group. Not an issue with the kayaks; they were all singles. But a big problem for this Swamp part of the trip. We would be paddling two-person canoes.

I noticed the oversight as our shuttle disappeared down Carter Road in a thick haze of dust. I looked at Kevin and winced. He didn't catch on until we got to pairing up paddling partners. It was funny to see him counting partners again and again, always of course coming up one short. Yep, we had an odd number of people. No cell phone to call our driver back. Wouldn't have mattered anyway. We were stuck with seven canoes and 13 people. I looked at Kevin's flushed face. He knew he had screwed up. Actually, it was my mistake for not double checking. But, as the true leader he would become, he took full responsibility and said he would paddle solo. I knew that wasn't a good idea and assigned myself the task.

But I wasn't relishing the prospect. Paddling 12 miles from Kingfisher Landing to Maul Hammock is a challenge even with a partner. Today would be an even bigger challenge for me as a solo paddler in a tandem 17.5' canoe loaded with my gear and our common gear. The canoe definitely needed to be paddled by two people.

To counter balance my non-existent partner, I decided to sit backwards in the bow seat to bring my weight more forward. Good thing I decided to do that. The wind blew relentlessly right into our faces the entire way. Had I sat in the stern, my bow would have been so elevated I would have been doing wheelies all day long or been blown off course or at least forced to make many more corrections than usual.

We loaded up. Me, myself, and I in the lead canoe. Kevin took the sweep position with Logan. Leah had waifish Joseph, and Nathan took on the smallest lad Royce. Against my better judgement, our spider-phobes, Marcus, tall, lanky, already sporting a scruffy, sparsely populated ginger beard, paired up with Josh, shorter, definitely more ample, dark-haired, dark dancing eyes. Equal-sized Chris and Jeremy paired up, as did Noah and Sam. We were off!

I paddled harder than perhaps I should have. Not wanting to slow our little flotilla, I set a good pace even for a tandem canoe, had I been with a partner. I really felt like paddling full bore and straight through to make sure we, well, I, made it to the platform before nightfall. But I forced myself to slow down to enjoy the gorgeous scenery and to share some points of interest with the boys.

Kids are especially interested in the weird and strange. Sex really gets their attention and scatology, poop, as well. I opted for strange and weird and concentrated on carnivorous plants and their interesting strategies.

Our first stop of interest – pitcher plants. *Sarracenia minor*, *Sarracenia psittacina* and *Sarracenia flava*. Hooded, parrot, and trumpet respectively. All the canoes bunched in to see the weird looking plants. Marcus and Josh pulled up behind Chris and Jeremy, followed by our sweep, Kevin and Logan. I stood up in my canoe so all the boys could hear me and see me pointing to the various parts of the plant. I held up a nearly dead but still greenish leaf as the example. Its long slender leaf folded and sealed along the long edge to form a narrow vase, a pitcher that holds liquid. A hood-like piece covered the top opening.

"These pitcher plants have a very interesting strategy for survival in this rather nutrient-poor substrate. Plants need nitrogen, and it's not available in this mostly anaerobic,

Hooded Pitcher Plants in Flower

Parrot Pitcher Plants with Flowers

low-oxygen soil. But they get around that hiccup by eating insects. Yep, think "Little Shop of Horrors" on a smaller scale. An irresistible scent is exuded on the upper, outer lip of the leaf. Flies, leaf hoppers, shield bugs, fill-in-the-blank insect name, just cannot resist that aroma. Like a moth to a flame they are drawn to that scent. Only problem is, if they go inside the lip, and they always do, they never get out."

I pointed to the lip with the inviting scent and pantomimed an insect struggling to get back out. My high-octane animated presentation with the broad expanse of gorgeous green prairie and brilliantly blue sky dotted with alabaster white cotton-puff clouds would have made an interesting posting on YouTube with the volume off. I am sure that, to an uninformed onlooker, I looked like a maniac.

"A mass of fine hair-like projections grow downward inside the vase-like leaf. Once in, the insect can't go back up against those downward-pointing hairs. To thwart even the cleverest insect though, pitcher plants have adapted over time. They have "windows" on the backside of the leaf. These windows, really just light areas in the green part of the leaf, trick the insect into thinking that there is a way out. It's just a cruel joke though. Eventually the insect wears out and falls to the bottom of the leaf. There in that bottom is the most incredibly efficient fast-acting digestive soup of enzymes. That insect that munched on another plant that had fixed nitrogen out of richer soil somewhere else, now supplies the pitcher plant with nitrogen and any other nutrients it picked up. Brilliant strategy, huh?"

My charges, duly impressed, immediately reached for a leaf themselves. I stopped them with the admonition that the Refuge particularly forbade such plucking even for educational purposes. Think if all canoeists did what we wanted to do. Instead I selected one nearly spent leaf for the educational sacrifice. I let Noah and Sam take charge of the dissection, and they gleefully rose to the occasion.

Noah pulled out a small pocket knife that he wasn't supposed to have. Leah and Nathan exchanged looks and shrugged it off. They could live with him breaking this rule especially since he assumed this teaching role so eagerly and seriously.

Sam prepared the paddle blade for the display and pulled out his pocket 20X microscope to examine the contents. I had equipped the boys with these essential powerful little tools prior to launching. Pleased, I smiled to see them employed carefully, thoughtfully, just like intended.

Sam passed the paddle with the dissected pitcher plant splayed open on its blade to the next canoe, and those kids passed it on to the next until each boy observed

Sundew Close-Up (Photo by Todd Mussman)

and investigated our small treasure as much as he wanted. I really liked these guys!

It's amazing what a trip into a wilderness area will do to precipitate pure spontaneous enjoyment and spark natural curiosity. Just below the surface there is always joy in discovery at any age.

As we prepared to continue on our way, I noticed Josh and Marcus smiling broadly. Could it be they were actually having a good time and relaxed too? Weren't these the same guys who didn't want to come to the Swamp in the first place? Well, I'll be damned! How 'bout them apples, as my father would say.

We paddled for a couple more miles until I spotted a swath of delicate little rosy-red drops glistening

Sundew

on the ends of sundew stalks. Those little rubies are sticky digestive enzymes, bad news for bugs. These plants are so tiny it takes a well-trained eye to spot them. We stopped. Noon already. I told everyone to eat the lunches we'd packed right before we launched. While everyone finished up, I used my paddle to scoop up an entire clump of peat with an intact diminutive sundew. I would replace the entire clump back to its original place when I finished chatting.

I find the small sundews, *Drosera intermedia*, almost always on peat blowups. When paddling the narrow trails through the prairies, I pay close attention to those blowups looking for the delicate rose-pink of the sundews. They are so small you have to scrutinize the blowups to pick them out. Once I point them out to my trip participants, the more eagle-eyed will be able to pick them out on their own. The others just wonder how in the heck we spot them from a moving canoe!

I stood up and began a Socratic style of inquiry. "So, what's the story here? Anyone want to venture a guess as to this plant's strategy for survival? You know it's a carnivore. I already told you that. So how does it make its living? Anyone?"

Noah wasted no time. Anointed with swamp water now, immersed in it, he launched into a stunningly accurate strategical description.

"So, just looking at these teeny tiny pink spikey things with the pink drops coming off the green pads, I'm guessing those drops do the dirty work. Right?"

"Yep, go on."

"So, so, the insect is attracted to the red drops, maybe it even tastes sweet or something and gets zapped." Noah accurately described the attraction mechanism.

"Yep, you're on a roll, man, and then what? How does the sundew digest the insect and where does the digested slurry go?"

"Hmmm, well, let's see. Do the leaves curl up around the insect?" Inspecting the sundew now with his pocket scope, he touched one of the stalked glands and to his delight it responded. His investigations targeted the heart of the strategy.

"Exactly!" I delivered my response with almost too much enthusiasm, momentarily teetering, I lost balance. Fortunately Kevin grabbed my gunnel and me. Good save. Nice kid. Excellent instincts. I straightened myself and regained my composure. How embarrassing that would have been to have thrown myself in the drink!

"That's it, exactly! The sundew's pink spikey things, actually stalked glands, on its little green leaf pad are extremely sensitive to touch. When an insect, attracted to the lovely rosy sweet droplets lands on that pad, it begins closing up. It's not the quick snap of a Venus flytrap. More like the slow motion of the tortoise in Aesop's famed fable. But those droplets are very sticky and don't let go. The sticky drops clog the insect's spiracles, its breathing apparatus, and in about 15 minutes the insect is toast. Another set of enzymes on the leaf pads then begins digestion. The nutritious insect slurry is then absorbed by other glands in the leaf pad. Voila! The nutrient cycle comes full circle. Fascinating, isn't it?"

Transfixed, my charges smiled goofily, completely caught up in the wonders of this tiny little plant, a power house in their active minds. Way cool!

I grabbed for a power bar since my energy levels all of a sudden dipped. Teaching solo and paddling solo zapped my energy big time.

We prepared to paddle on. But not before Josh and Marcus asked if they could be last in our little flotilla.

"Really? Wow! That's great y'all want to be in the sweep, but nope. No can do. Kevin and Logan are sweep and y'all need to stay in front of them. Next to last."

We paddled on. What change had occurred to prompt that request from those two?

The wind really picked up, and I struggled to keep the canoe on course. Each stroke forward followed by two corrective strokes. Exhausting day, but exhilarating too. The boys enjoyed this place and the remarkable transformation in Marcus and Josh simply astounded me. Leah and Nathan too were very pleased.

At mile marker eleven we stopped, more for myself than the boys. They seemed as if they could easily sprint the rest of the way. Teenage boys have an endless reserve of energy. I on the other hand pushed a loaded canoe into the wind by myself. Lots of energy expended. Not easy, but doable, obviously doable.

I stopped to point out the bladderworts. My favorite little carnivores. In the fall a few yellow bladderworts are still blooming. I pointed to them. Again using the Socratic Method, I asked them to investigate the plants with their whorls of leaves that looked like delicate frilly green doilies floating right beneath the surface. Some had stalks with canary-yellow flowers sticking bolt upright from the center of those floating doilies. In the Swamp there are several species of bladderworts. We observed the yellow, *Utricularia inflata*. I asked them to come up with an explanation for how the teeny tiny little bladders I pointed out, could possibly be used to eat an insect.

Again, I smiled at their creative thoughtfulness.

Jeremy, our buddying engineer, wasted no time. "So are these little bladders pressure sensitive?"

"Yep, and so, how does that help the hungry little bladderwort capture its meal?"

All the others pulled out their pocket scopes too. This query required serious investigation at the microscopic level, now that they knew the point of focus. The tiny little bladders served not only as flotation devices, but somehow also in the feeding process.

Yellow Bladderworts (*Utricularia inflata*)

177

Jeremy continued his deductive reasoning, "So, there has to be a trigger that explodes the bladder to capture the insect. Right?"

"Trigger, yes, explosion, no. Try again."

Jeremy scrunched his nose and dug deeper. The wheels in his head churned. Smoke wafted out of his ears. He concentrated. Then. Eureka!

"Oh, oh, wait! No explosion, but how 'bout an implosion?"

"Ding, ding, ding! Bingo! You, young sir, get a gold star affixed to the very center of your forehead for such good sleuthing!"

I really did carry a pad of gold stars with me. In grammar school one of my teachers affixed gold stars to our foreheads to clearly designate us as stellar students. To all our classmates, schoolmates, parents, other kids' parents, the whole world, if the stars stayed affixed long enough. A good incentivizing strategy to be sure, I employed it myself, because it worked, at any age.

Zebra Butterfly on Tickseed Sunflowers

Lily Pads in Dinner Pond on Red Trail

Much to everyone's surprise I fished around in my daypack and pulled out a well-traveled pad of gold stars. Jeremy proudly sported his until it would stick no longer. Even big kids love to be special. Even with simple goofy little gold stars affixed to the middle of their foreheads.

"Okay, gentlemen and lady." A nod to Leah. "Just one more mile to go! This has been a hard day of paddling against the wind, and we approach our day's end. You dear sirs, and lady, are Rock Stars! Congratulations! Let's roll!"

"Wait, wait!" Josh pleaded loudly. "Please, please, Miss Cathy, Marcus and I really want to paddle last. Please, please, pretty please with sugar on it?"

Wow, I hadn't heard that kind of begging since, well, since I couldn't remember when. And this from my two who didn't want to come to the Swamp in the first place. I looked over at Kevin, Leah, and Nathan to

179

determine their comfort level with this request. They shrugged okay. I gave strict instruction.

"Gentlemen, your teachers and your leaders are giving you this one time, and one time only, dispensation. You will keep Kevin and Logan in sight at all times. Their canoe will be in front of you. You will not dawdle. You will arrive at Maul Hammock platform by 5:00 PM. It is now 4:15. It should only take you 20 minutes at most to paddle this last mile. I understand you want to experience the Swamp on your own, and I applaud you for that. We all applaud you for embracing this experience. You must also understand that we are responsible for you and the rest of the group. Should you not show up at the appointed time we will send a search party for you, and we will not be pleased. This kind of diversion could compromise the safety and enjoyment of this experience for all us. Do you understand me?"

"Yes, Ma'am! Yes, Ma'am!" They actually saluted. Hmmm, I guess I could be authoritative if I put my mind to it. Who knew?

I led off our little flotilla with steady even strokes. Tired, I still had enough oomph in me to make this last mile without too much effort. I should have eaten another power bar, but I didn't take the time. Silly me. I strained a bit against the wind but kept up a good pace right up to Maul Hammock. I must admit though I smiled broadly, very relieved, when I saw that bent up turbine atop the privy twirling to beat the band in that strong wind.

Only those who know to look for the turbine will see it. At this time the entire platform at Maul Hammock was hidden by lots of thick shrubs, bushes, and small trees. You were on it before you really saw it. Some have paddled right on past it and been surprised when they turned around to see it behind them. This platform was rebuilt in a new location after it burned in the great Okefenokee fires that raged from late summer 2011 and continued through late spring 2012.

As soon as I came alongside the small landing dock, I hopped out and unloaded my gear and the common gear to make room for the canoe behind me. I moved quickly and efficiently. Like a well-run depot, the canoes arrived one behind the other with enough time in between arrivals for the canoes to be emptied of gear and moved before the next one arrived. We worked together like long-practiced baggage handlers at Delta's enormous Atlanta hub. We anticipated each other's moves instinctively and in very short order our neat little tent city sprang up on that small platform with the kitchen set up to one side.

All of the sudden though, my head spun, and I felt myself sinking. Literally. I found one of the shelter's posts that held up the corrugated tin roof and slid right down it, sitting on the platform with my back against that pole, my knees in my chest. My blood glucose level had plummeted from the over expenditure of energy of paddling and moving gear. I had not consumed enough calories during the last part of the day. I shook uncontrollably. Kevin came over to the gear boxes near me to get extra line for a tent. His foot came just close enough for me to pound one fist on it. He bent down to my face and screamed.

"Oh, My God, You're not going to die on me, are you???"

I had forgotten to mention to Kevin I had been recently diagnosed as hypoglycemic and that I controlled it quite nicely with lots of snacks throughout the day and a little capsule of vanadium sulfate at each big meal. Peter Brodhead and his wife Janie owned the original local health food store in Savannah called Brighter Day. Peter trained to be a naturopathic doctor. After the diagnosis from my regular physician, I consulted with Peter, who set me on a course of these little magical pills.

Diabetes is in my genetic ancestry on both sides, and I most likely would be a full-blown diabetic by now were it not for Peter and these magical little mineral capsules. Turns out pigs also regularly succumb to diabetes, and vanadium sulfate is added to their commercial feed to prevent it.

I hissed in a whisper, "Shut up! Shut up. Just get me some sugar. Now!"

Flummoxed, Kevin, not in control of his terror and not understanding my condition, shouted, "Sugar? Sugar? Where do I get sugar?"

"Kevin, listen to me, calm down! No one else needs to know. Just bring me a cookie or candy bar, anything with sugar."

Kevin twirled around to the food box, flipped open the latches and ripped off the lid. He riffled through the box and hit the bag of Oreos first. Good choice. He ripped open the bag and grabbed six cookies. He spun back around to me and tried to stuff all six into my mouth. I had just enough energy to thwart that choking disaster. I took one and slowly let it melt in my mouth with some under my tongue.

I usually enjoyed the heck out of Oreos by dipping them in hot black coffee, letting them linger for just a minute to dissolve slightly, and then delighting as the soft almost oozing black chocolate melded into that white creamy center, now flavored with a hint of bitter black coffee. Yum. I have enjoyed this method from childhood. My dear, indulgent, tolerant parents who drank only black coffee allowed me to dip my Oreos into their unviolated coffee. I never acquired a taste for coffee nor a need for its caffeine. Not even in college.

Not even in grad school. But I still sure do enjoy Oreos dipped in black coffee when someone will allow the indulgence.

At this moment I desperately needed the sugar of that Oreo to bring my blood glucose level up. Up to where my brain could function and I could regain control of my muscles. My mind started down too many dark thought tunnels it couldn't complete. My body remained unresponsive to my mind's commands to move. Tears welled up uncontrollably in my eyes and spilled down my cheeks. I barely had enough energy to pull my baseball cap down over my face so no one would see my desperate situation.

The boys, Leah, and Nathan buzzed around the platform oblivious to my situation. Kevin diverted attention from me by busying himself at the kitchen and occasionally bending down to ostensibly take direction while I "rested". In about 15 minutes I could feel the Oreo working. In another few minutes I could concentrate, and then the shaking stopped and the tears dried up. I was back! I slowly worked my way up the pole to a standing position and, like a person trying to walk for the first time after being bed-ridden for months, I carefully, cautiously, stepped away from the support of the pole. Right foot. Left foot. Good. Standing with no support. No shaking. Whew, that was close!

I quickly caught Kevin up on my medical situation and promised to monitor myself better. He apologized for the dramatic outburst, and I apologized for forgetting to tell him in the first place. I really thought I had it under control.

Leah noticed Kevin and I chatting and came over to confer. She pointed to her watch indicating that Josh and Marcus should be arriving soon. Right on cue we heard their voices in the distance. Relieved, we relaxed.

Small hollies, hurrah bush, and wax myrtles bordered Maul Hammock platform on three of its four sides. The fourth side facing east opened out on to Maul Hammock Lake. The canoe trail approached the platform from the north. You could not see approaching canoes but you could hear the paddlers as they chatted to one other. Their voices increasing in volume the closer they neared the platform.

Josh and Marcus' chattering increased as did their giggles. Funny how much they sounded like teenage girls when they giggled. Their paddles banged the gunnels as they made their way ever closer. Leah, Kevin, Nathan, and I decided to stand on the landing dock to welcome them and congratulate them on embracing the Swamp experience so whole heartedly and for being on time.

While waiting for them, we busied ourselves by deciding who among the boys would help with dinner and who with cleanup. We assigned ourselves chores, and my dear colleagues sweetly exempted me from any duties since I soloed the entire day and would do the same for the next two days. I gratefully accepted their magnanimous gesture of kindness. My sleeping bag would feel wonderful tonight.

Josh and Marcus neared, their voices ever louder. Giggling uncontrollably now with an inside joke no doubt. They were Swamp Hollering!

Marcus sang out in a Tarzan-like call. "Ahh, Eeeahh, Eeeahh, Eeeahh, Eeeahh!"

Josh answered with his call, more musical, almost a yodel. Quite creative. "Ahhheeeooooah, Ahhheeeooooah, Ahhheeeooooah, Ahhheeeooooah!"

Fabulous! These guys embraced every aspect of the Swamp experience now. Wow, they really had done a complete 180! Good for them!

Maul Hammock Lake View from New Platform

Leah said, "I cannot believe our biggest complainers are the very ones now Swamp Hollering like Tarzan the Ape Man, in the middle of the big bad awful scary Okefenokee Swamp, no less."

"Yeah, amazing, isn't it?" Nathan added, also in disbelief. "This is quite the major U-turn."

Kevin pondered, "What do you suppose got in to them? Oh no, drugs? You think?"

Leah answered the question, "No, we searched and patted down all the boys' belongings and gear and clothing, everything, thoroughly for weed and drugs before we left school and again at that hotel. They couldn't have gotten into any of that. Unless they found something natural along the way. And they wouldn't know what that would be anyway. I think they're just on a natural Swamp high."

"Well, they haven't used the chemical toilet yet where the big bad black widows bite your ass when you sit." We all laughed.

Kevin, ever the jokester added, "Yeah, maybe I'll put my plastic spider in the privy in the morning."

"Yes, yes, yes - no, no, no!" But it certainly would be entertaining.

Josh and Marcus' Swamp Hollers rang out just on the other side of the holly tree wall. They were right there. We could have poked our arms through the wall of leaves and touched them.

I heard the water swoosh as their paddles moved the canoe forward.

The nose of their forest-green canoe peaked past the tree-line.

We beamed, delighted that they completely embraced this Swamp experience. We clapped to welcome them home.

Josh's paddle broke the water. The forward momentum carried him into view. His bare arm, his bare chest, his bare leg, his bare head, his.... Standing straight up in the bow, he turned his head as he came into full view. At the sight of us standing on the dock, a look of horror broke across his face. He was in full view. In Full Monty, full view.

Our mouths dropped open.

Another stroke of their paddles, the canoe glided forward revealing Marcus also standing, in full view. In Full Monty, full view.

Leah and I both reflexively spun on our heels. We gasped. Female eyes averted.

Marcus and Josh gasped, sat down quickly, too quickly, and yelped. Tarzan gone.

Nathan gasped. We hadn't, as leaders, role played this scenario.

Kevin guffawed, caught himself, and gasped in solidarity with us adults.

The other boys literally shook the platform as they jumped around doubled over in hysterics. They rioted at the sight of their bare brethren. They went berserk.

It took a few long seconds for us leaders to get over the shock. But Nathan and Kevin mercifully and authoritatively took control.

Leah and I, helpless, shielded our delicate feminine eyes from the manly display, our backs still turned to the Full Monty Brothers.

Oh My God! I had never encountered a situation like this before. As funny as it was, these were kids, minors. Oh Dear! The implications were very serious. Nudity was not mentioned in the leader protocol guide book.

I looked at Leah and began to verbalize the next steps. She preempted me.

"We'll handle this one, Cathy. We have strict rules for these types of situations, and the boys will suffer the school's consequences. There will be lots of demerits and groundings."

"I'll have to file a full report. Certainly the consequences are yours to mete out. But I have to say, this is a first for me!" I chuckled. "I just can't believe it!"

Leah allowed herself to laugh too. "Damn, I thought I had seen it all! But good for Josh and Marcus for going native! Can you believe it? Those two went native!"

We chalked it up to the primeval spell and natural charm of the Great Okefenokee Swamp. Fairly harmless, though, I am quite sure their story was told over and over again and will be told in the hallowed halls of their school for many years hence. The trip the Full Monty Swamp Brothers experienced Going Native.

Swamp Water Skies (Photo by Jody Patterson)

CHAPTER 8

OKE VIP

Spring 1986

It's not every day a working naturalist is called to action with a rather cryptic request. It was a Monday evening, April 1986.

"It's your turn to answer the phone."

"Nope. Pretty sure it's yours. Remember your mother called, and I answered and then ended up talking to her for over an hour?"

"Oh yeah, right," he reflected. Crawfish reluctantly reached for the phone I politely but insistently held out to him.

"Hello? Yep, this is Crawfish. Oh hello, Bob. Yeah, how's it going? Hmmm. Ah ha. Well. Well. Ah ha. Yep, of course! Yeah, sure! We'll do it! Just let us know the exact day and time you want us there. Yep, good. Okay, please give Linda our love. Okay, talk ta ya soon!"

Crawfish, still holding the phone in his giant paw, placed the receiver back in its cradle. Then ran his strong thick fingers through the mass of dark unruly curls that sprang out in corkscrewed coils all over his head.

"That was Bob Kerr of the Georgia Conservancy. He wants us to go with him and Linda on a VIP trip through the Swamp. We'll most likely go in this Friday or Saturday. We'll be staying at the VIP cabin on Big Water!"

"Wow! I've always wanted to stay in that VIP cabin! Who's the VIP?"

"Didn't say. Just this is very top secret until we meet everyone involved on the day we go in. We just have to wait for the next call telling us when and where."

This was all very cloak and dagger. How often do you get to guide an unknown person with enough clout to secure a trail through the Swamp with only a few days' notice and get to stay in the very exclusive VIP Cabin?

For the next three days every time the phone rang both of us jumped to answer it. There was no "It's your turn." "Nope, pretty sure it's yours." Now we were racing to reach the phone first. Moving around the house like waiting for the music to stop in a game of musical chairs. Every time the phone rang, we sprang.

Crawfish, John Anthony Crawford, my husband, was the first professional naturalist I had ever met. He remains my greatest mentor. We married in early May 1976 while I still attended classes, finishing up my Bachelor of Science in Biology at Armstrong State University. We met in the fall of the previous year after a mutual friend invited him to our weekly evenings of playing volleyball, drinking beer, and eating potluck college student fare in my back yard. When we met, we were like two insects whose antennae locked on to each other's pheromone trails and never unlocked. We had a whirlwind courtship of just a few months and stayed married until 1989, remaining friends ever since.

The anxiously awaited second call finally came. Crawfish reached the phone first, snatching up the receiver from underneath my open palm in mid-grab.

"Hey, Bob, been waitin' on ya ta call. Yep. Okay. Got it. Yep, we'll be there!"

That Friday afternoon we were to meet in Folkston for dinner with Superintendent of the Okefenokee National Wildlife Refuge John Schroer and his wife Becky and Bob and his Atlanta-based attorney wife Linda DiSantis and our still unknown VIP. We would spend the night in the only hotel in Folkston, a one level, run down, but still functioning motel called The Tahiti Motel, and depart the next morning for our one-night VIP foray into the Swamp. This was so thrilling and quite special and very hush hush! G A Confidential.

For young naturalists on bare-bones incomes,

John "Crawfish" Crawford & Jeana Aquadro Crawford

deciding what to wear on a VIP trip had us both on edge. Well, one of us anyway. Crawfish had a much more limited wardrobe than I did and really didn't care about clothes nor making an impression. His wardrobe consisted of holey blue jeans, even holier T-shirts with lots of stains, and a few flannel long-sleeved shirts for colder days. He did have a very nice, very stylish, very practical, navy blue wool pea coat left over from his time in the Navy.

I, on the other hand, had been courted by seven out of nine high-school sororities in Nashville and had been sent to Charm School to learn societal etiquette. Yes, there really was such an institution, and my mother really did send me to it in seventh grade. I knew the ropes when it came to high society. I surmised our VIP was of very high social standing. My social training would be put to good use. Thank You, Mother!

I selected my clothes for our two-day trip carefully. A very nice set of casual dinner clothes and two sets of my very best field clothes. In early April we would enjoy warm days and chilly nights just right for sleeping. To be sure, that's the best time to be in the Swamp, but I put in a few extra things for the chill just in case.

Crawfish threw a T-shirt and long sleeved flannel shirt into a small canvas bag lined with a plastic bag to keep the contents dry. That was it. In a matter of seconds he had packed. I always admired the simplicity of his wardrobe except on those occasions when a clean shirt and unwrinkled pants would have been nice.

I barely remember the drive down to Folkston. We had both done it so many times the VW van could have driven itself. We led many field trips to the Okefenokee during spring and fall, our busiest times in the Swamp. What I always look for and expect this time of year is the I-95 median to be ablaze in crimson with the blooming of the same-named clover.

We reached the Schroer's home, just outside the city limits of Folkston, around 5:00 PM. A nice house, a brick rancher, with a wraparound porch appropriately populated with two whitewashed rocking chairs. Becky came out of the house to greet us and then ushered us into the living room where Bob and Linda chatted with her husband John and our VIP.

They all stood up upon our entry. The VIP extended his hand.

Crawfish took Senator Sam Nunn's hand first, squeezing a bit too hard and pumping it a bit too rapidly. Sam winced and immediately tried to disengage from Crawfish's vice-like grip. Crawfish instinctively gave Michelle Nunn, the Senator's daughter, a big bear hug.

I think I almost curtsied but caught myself before I made that amateur mistake. All big teeth smiles, I said, "I'm a big fan, er, rather supporter, er, I voted for you!"

Sam chuckled good-naturedly, as did everyone else.

Senator Sam Nunn! Senior senator from Georgia and the powerful Chair of the Senate's Committee on Armed Services. Already being talked about as the next Democratic Presidential candidate.

With him his oldest child, Michelle, a freshman in college who had always wanted to go through the Okefenokee Swamp. Apparently her dad did too.

The rest of that afternoon we discussed all sorts of issues in the Schroer's living room. Bob dominated the conversation with politics, putting forth his agenda on behalf of the Georgia Conservancy. All important stuff to be sure. Crawfish and I grew antsy. As people of the outdoors, naturalists, we had been summoned to do a job, and we wanted to talk Swamp.

Finally, mercifully, Becky announced dinner was on the table. We all eagerly bee-lined it for the table. Nothing like heady political conversation to work up your appetite. There spread before us large, sweating glasses of sweet ice tea; thick rose-pink slices of smoked ham; dark, thin redeye gravy made the traditional way with coffee and pan drippings; a large bowl piled high with still-steaming white rice; another large bowl of hot black-eyed peas; another of bright, fresh green beans; and a very large bowl of iceberg lettuce with tomatoes and cucumbers fresh from Becky's already-producing garden.

All topped off with incredibly delicious homemade peach cobbler made with frozen Georgia peaches from last year's crop and capped off with a large scoop of vanilla ice cream. I lapped that up, even though I don't usually indulge if it's not chocolate, dark chocolate to be exact.

With our bellies full and only 6:30 PM, I mentally groaned, knowing we had a long night ahead of us. With this very high-caloric overload in my system I would soon be struggling to keep my eyes open. Sure enough, I embarrassingly nodded off as soon as I sank into that cushy love seat next to Crawfish.

The drone of Bob's low nearly monotone gravelly voice, punctuated with John's excited Yankee clipped speech pattern, and the occasional addition of Sam's soft gentlemanly southern drawl lulled me to sleep like a child being read a good bedtime story, with mom changing voices for each character.

Periodically I received a little jab to the ribs. Snorting in response. How very embarrassing. Michelle and Becky found my situation quite amusing, chuckling, exchanging sideways glances and snickers with each other. I know how I must have looked. Ridiculous.

Gator Sentry at Entrance to Purple Trail in Chase Praire

I wondered how in the world a Senator did this all the time. I imagined night after night of banal, small-talk dinner parties and endless fact-loaded meetings. The norm for Senator Sam. Not for me. A child of the outdoors, I wanted no part of this lifestyle. Get me out of here!

I nodded off again.

Crawfish, annoyed, a bit forcefully propped me up against the armrest to free his arm so he could worm his way into the conversation. His loud booming voice rang out straight into my right ear. Startled awake, I snorted. Embarrassed again. I wiped my mouth. I had drooled. Even more embarrassing. Becky and Michelle were beside themselves in hysterics, and now so was Linda. I don't think Sam, Bob, nor John had noticed yet.

"So tomorrow, what's the plan, John? Cathy and I are ready to give Senator Sam and Michelle our best Swamp experience."

"Right." Superintendent John Schroer grateful for the

invitation to speak, "We'll eat breakfast here and then head over to the Refuge Visitor Center, so Michelle and Sam can get a feel for what they'll experience through the displays. While they're doing that, you and Cathy can fill them in on what to expect. I'll get the boats ready and then we'll launch around 10:00 AM."

"Okay, great! So, we'll...." Crawfish began, but Bob cut him short, turning the conversation right back to bending Senator Sam's ear. Sam scowled. So did everyone else as we were sucked back into political conversation mode.

At one point Sam managed to gain control of the floor long enough to ask Becky what she did. Becky wasted no time at all bending Sam's other ear about the plight of school teachers in the state of Georgia and especially in Charlton County, one of the poorest counties in the state. Sam promised to help improve those schools and raise teacher salaries. Becky beamed, very pleased. I was impressed that she had the guts to bring up the issue in the first place and that she had launched right into it. She wasted no time with small talk. She knew that, if she didn't get to her issue right out of the gate, she might not have a chance otherwise. That night lots of issues floated in the air of their comfortable, middle-class living room.

I really didn't sleep that night. Sleeping in a moldy, rundown hotel for one night is not comfortable. Knowing what the next day would bring even more challenging. Crawfish snored so loudly the dead would have had trouble sleeping their eternal sleep. Of course earlier I had no trouble at all nodding off with a full belly in a warm living room with droning voices. Funny how that works.

The next morning dawned bright and sunny and warm. The dew, still glistening on the grass blades on the Schroer's lawn, wet our shoes as we walked across it to enter Chez Shroer for breakfast.

Shortly, Becky summoned us to her dining room table where she had spread a fine country style breakfast on her red checkerboard tablecloth, much like my grandmother's tasty mornings. Becky's table nearly overflowed again with food – bright yellow scrambled eggs, crisp bacon and juicy sausage, hot homemade cathead biscuits piled high with a jar of amber tupelo honey next to it. Fortified, we could now endure a long day of paddling. And by my calculations, this was going to be a very long day of paddling. I must have nodded off when John detailed the plans of the next day at the dinner party.

As scheduled, we arrived at the Okefenokee National Wildlife Refuge Visitor Center and dutifully engaged Sam, Michelle, Bob, and Linda while Superintendent John disappeared to ready our canoes and gear. Crawfish's voice reverberated throughout the small, very well appointed visitor's center. My ears began to ache as they always did when he was excited, and he was very excited.

Information poured out of Crawfish like an out-of-control gushing geyser. After only a few minutes I could see our guests' eyes beginning to glaze over with the overload of information. When presenting to an audience of any size, you must gauge how you are being received. Crawfish never really got the hang of that. He had so much information bottled up in his head that it spilled out all the time. Regardless of the situation. He just couldn't help it. Most of the time it fell on appreciative ears, filling receptive, inquisitive minds.

Michelle and Sam moved away from him in retreat, and he moved reflexively to their sides. Quite humorous to watch. An awkward dance of sorts.

Fortunately this pas de trois only lasted a short while,

ending when Superintendent John came through the door. We all turned to him for grateful relief from the overload of information already filling up our heads and assaulting our ears.

We walked down to the waiting van and loaded our gear into it. I saw no canoe trailer nor any canoes on top of the van. Hmmm. Once seated and strapped in, we headed off for Kingfisher Landing 21 miles north of Folkston.

Crawfish continued to expound on the virtues of the Swamp, and at some point Bob actually said, "Stop! Stop! Please! John needs to speak to Sam about a few things, and this will be his last chance to do that. You'll have Sam's ear for the next 24 hours." Crawfish sat back and frowned like a reprimanded kid.

For a half hour we bounced along the several miles of deep-sand, washboard-bumpy Carter Drive (yep, one of President Jimmy's kin), kicking up a high plume of dust. Out our dust-hazed windows we observed the modern-day turpentining technique of screwing empty two-liter plastic Coke or Pepsi bottles into the base of pine trees to collect the sap.

Turpentining had come a long way since the days of slashing cathead cuts into the bases of the trees and affixing tin funnel trays to direct the dripping sap into collection buckets. No matter how you did it, it was still a very sticky business.

With our livers, bowels, and kidneys thoroughly shaken, yet thankfully still intact, we arrived at Kingfisher Landing. There to my great surprise loomed two giant airboats! "For us?" I asked in disbelief.

"Yep, your Swamp chariots." John replied, smiling at my surprise. "You six will ride with me on this one, and Hank here will transport your three canoes and gear on the other."

How absolutely thrilling! At this point in my career I had not been on an airboat. I had heard them in the Everglades and thought them an abomination, a hazard to wildlife. I hadn't considered that they could actually be useful tools. They were definitely going to be useful today.

I had been having a really hard time understanding how we were going to paddle to Maul Hammock from Kingfisher today, 12 miles, and then on to the VIP cabin in Big Water, another 11 or so miles. By my calculations that would be over 23 miles of paddling. I knew I would be tired, and, looking at Michelle and Sam and Linda and Bob, I guessed that it would be way too much for them to paddle in one day. Crawfish on the other hand would relish it....as a warm up.

We piled into the airboat with John at the stick. We buckled up, donned life preservers, and placed hearing protection muffs over our ears. This was, after all, just an airplane engine mounted on the back of a flat-bottomed shallow-draft scow. Airboats are very tricky to operate, and many an inexperienced operator, going full-tilt boogie, have tipped these puppies over, without a good ending.

We however were safe in the hands of our local experts. These refuge managers used their airboats as tools to maintain and clear trails, hunt for overdue paddlers, evacuate sick ones, haul supplies and materials to repair platforms, transport tanks to honey-dip chemical toilets, etc. Thankfully they knew what they were doing.

Superintendent John looked around at us to make sure our ear-protecting muffs were in place and our belts buckled. He nodded to each of us as an okay, twisted back around in his seat, and fired up the engine. It was loud!

The blades rotated slowly at first and then ramped up

Golden Clubs on Red Trail

their revolutions to take-off speed. And we took off!

The ride through Carters Prairie's vast vista, incredibly breath-taking.

We skimmed and skipped along over the surface of the narrow black-water trails, twisting this way and that along the sinuous route. What a way to see the prairie!

In remarkably short order we saw the side trail to Double Lakes. Fragrant white water lilies parted as our zippy craft moved them aside. The ones directly in our path quickly slipped underneath, resurfacing as we passed over them. We careened headlong in a real live, time-lapse Okefenokee video travelogue. What a thrill!

John and Hank expertly urged their airboats through snaking narrow waterways. In a few areas hurrah bush and sweetspire and titi scratched the hulls. Singing the Swamp's siren song. Like playing a familiar record at intermittent speeds.

We couldn't talk. We wouldn't have been able to hear each other. So we sat mute, enjoying the striking, streaking visuals before us. What a glorious way to experience the Swamp, albeit way too loud. Each in our own delightful heady worlds. Each enjoying the gorgeous sights flying by us. Each enjoying the one and only, The Great Okefenokee Swamp.

In sharp contrast, on most of my trips, I select a place where I instruct my group to get comfortable. If in canoes, we tie bow or stern off to a log or stump and secure anything that will move. Our goal, to sit with eyes closed for several minutes to just listen to the natural sounds. We slow down. We stop. Often this is one of the highlights by trip's end. Our busy lives are rarely free of human-made sounds, even for a few minutes.

While filming nature programs, we always find it very difficult to record outside. Rarely is there absence of human-made sounds. Most of the time we sit idle, waiting for a quiet break to record for just a few precious minutes of natural sound.

Even in the very heart of the Everglades and the Okefenokee you hear airplanes and jets and airboats. I've heard semis, chain saws, and train whistles. In other areas, you hear barking dogs, leaf blowers, car engines, motorcycles, garbage trucks, ambulance and police sirens, rifle and gun shots, boom boxes, etc. We exist in a very noisy society, and it is very hard to get away from our noise. Try to do it sometime. You will hear what I mean.

When leading a group of paddlers down a particularly lovely stretch in the Okefenokee such as Minnie's Lake Run or River Narrows or the eastern approach to Floyd's Island, I spread the canoes out and ask the paddling partners not to talk, to just enjoy the visuals and the natural sounds. That experience is another often referenced trip highlight. It is a very reverent experience, for some even spiritual.

John and Hank pushed their throttles forward to pick

up speed. We screamed down the canoe paths. No time to stop to admire the gorgeous rose pogonia orchids. They blurred by in a smear of streaking pink. Later we would do them justice.

Soon we zoomed into and out of Pond Lake, then Christmas Lake and then very soon after that Ohio Lake. We zipped through these three lakes barely discernable as such except for the signs that indicated you were actually in these areas. Each time we slowed down and sped up, the roar of the engine responded accordingly.

John and Hank skillfully nosed their bows into each turn so that the stern stayed in the waterway. We tipped up to the left and then rocked to the right. Each side taking turns being above those seated on the opposite side. I was giddy. What a very cool way to see the Swamp! No shoulder pain from paddling long distances. But then everything blurred by in an abstract painting of the natural realistic landscape I knew as my Swamp, and it was WAY TOO LOUD!!!

In an hour and a half I spotted the vent of the chemical

Gator in Grass

toilet on Maul Hammock platform glinting in the sun as it twirled in response to the differing temperatures inside and outside of the small essential enclosure. John pulled back on the throttle slowing his airboat and brought it to an expertly timed stop.

The airboat dwarfed the small dock meant for much lower-profile canoes. John hopped off to secure the bow line, removing his ear muffs in the process, which prompted us to do the same, life vests too. Superintendent John Schroer, ever the gentleman, held out his hand in support as we rocked the tippy airboat each time one of us stepped on the gunnel to disembark.

"Wow!" Everyone uttered the same exclamation. That one simple expression properly summed up what we all just collectively experienced. "Wow!"

"Welcome to Maul Hammock platform everyone!" John made a courtly bow for dramatic emphasis. It worked. We all smiled. "This is where I leave you in the hands of Crawfish and Cathy to experience the largest population of American alligators in the one and only, World-Famous Okefenokee Swamp!"

Even though a career federal refuge manager, John still appreciated this fabulous wilderness he managed. He knew how very special it was, and he gratefully, happily savored his work here every day. He bid us adieu and good paddling and then hopped back onboard his airboat to allow Hank to pull up with the canoes. Hank and Crawfish set about untying and then launching them on to the dark, mirrored-surface. Our fabulous day had already begun!

As soon as the noise of the large engines faded enough for us to hear one another, Crawfish took charge.

"Okay, so here's how we'll pair up. I'll paddle with Senator Sam, and Cathy with Michelle. I assume, Bob and Linda, y'all want to paddle together? Sam and I will be in the lead, and Bob and Linda in the sweep, and..."

"Er, hold up there, Crawfish," Senator Sam held up his hand like a schoolboy for permission to interrupt the no-room-for-interruption spiel. "Michelle and I will paddle together. We haven't spent much time with each other since she went off to college, and this trip is to be our father-daughter bonding time."

"Oh, uh, well then, okay, Bob and I'll paddle together in the lead with Cathy and Linda in the sweep." Crawfish just didn't miss a beat with this stuff.

"Hold on there, partner." Now Bob chimed in to protest the arrangements. "Linda and I'll paddle together, and you and Cathy can paddle together. And it doesn't matter if you're in the lead or not, we'll hear you no matter where you are!"

Bob looked down and shook his head in good humor, remembering another trip he had experienced with Crawfish loudly delivering a non-stop running narrative.

Bob, a very outgoing person who learned over the years to be diplomatic with his statements, typically led all meetings and get-togethers and didn't mince words.

Actually, everyone on this trip took charge most of their working days. Linda DiSantis, a high-profile Atlanta lawyer, tended to work on environmental issues. Later Linda would go on to become the Attorney for the City of Atlanta, after that General Counsel of CARE USA, and after that an esteemed university professor.

I led trips and assumed command on those trips except when co-leading with Crawfish. Crawfish overshadowed all of his co-leaders. When with him I got the "oh, so, you're the little wife" assessment.

Big Water Platform Northward View

That made my stomach churn more than anything. True, definitely smaller than Crawfish, as 99% of people were. And we were married. But no need to refer to me as his "little wife". In the South the context is "she made him a good little wife". Argh! As co-leader and naturalist in my own right, I had earned my own reputable credentials.

Crawfish had a lot more field experience than I did, but I also had a lot more academic training that I brought to the trips. He looked the part with his large muscular frame and mass of curls and burly beard. I looked like I stepped out of some chic boutique outdoor clothing catalog. Instead of the usual neutral tones typically worn by guides including Crawfish, I had a colorful wardrobe of teals and purples that at one point included 22 bathing suits with matching bandanas, ergo the nickname Neon Naturalist. On this trip, I opted for sea foam green.

Michelle, a lovely young woman just barely in college, would go on to assume many high-profile positions. Most notably she directed former President George H. W. Bush's Thousand Points of Light Foundation for several years. In 2015 she ran as the Democratic candidate for Georgia's US Senate seat. Even though she and her team fought gallantly and respectfully, they could not overcome the decades-long stronghold of the well-established and well-oiled Republican machine. At this point though she had the least person-in-charge attitude.

With our canoes packed, the appropriate partners climbed into their respective seats. I sat in the bow of our canoe, a real treat. When I lead a group, I paddle in the stern, usually with the least experienced paddler in my bow.

With Crawfish in the stern I had a real human powered 1000-horsepower motor on the back of our canoe. Incredibly strong, he often didn't know just how strong. I wouldn't be tired physically, but I knew my ears would be, so I had already prepared for his booming voice barking out a non-stop natural history narrative.

As soon as we launched, sure enough, Crawfish wasted not a single minute. He twisted and turned in his seat to project his voice just so. He wanted to make sure he did his job of informing and regaling Senator Sam, Michelle, Linda, and Bob with the wonders of the Okefenokee. Only five minutes into paddling though, Bob just couldn't take it anymore.

"Hey, look, man, we know you really want to share the Swamp with us, and there's so much you want us to know and see, but this is really not what we had in mind. Sam wants to spend time talking with Michelle, and I want to be able to hear my lovely bride. How 'bout we stop at points along the way for show-and-tell and questions, and you can dazzle us then? Deal?"

I was grateful. Having already suggested that way of imparting information, Crawfish would not to listen to me. After all, I was "the little wife".

Before the first paddle stroke, I had dug out two squares of toilet paper, wet them in inky Swamp water, squeezed them out a bit, and stuffed them in my ears. I learned to do this at rock concerts years ago when the music blasted out at deafening levels I just couldn't enjoy. Wet toilet paper in my ears reduced the noise to just the right comfort level.

"Uh, okay, no problem. Atchy and I'll paddle up ahead and stop in a little while."

He called me by my family nickname. Atchy. It stuck when, at the age of three, I managed to get all the letters in my name correct, just not in the right order.

Crawfish, his nickname, came from his proficiency with animals. At a very young age he demonstrated his budding naturalist skills. Kids around his neighborhood brought him injured animals, and he tenderly cared for them. Early on they called him "Lizard Doctor". Later he became known as Crawfish, that one stuck.

Crawfish and I had a lovely paddle together. We chatted easily, and I gladly removed the wads of wet toilet paper from my ears. No need for him to regale me with natural history information, although we did discuss mutual points of interest. I brought in physiology. I loved knowing how animals and plants adapted to certain conditions and their strategies to survive and thrive. I especially delighted in the survival strategies of carnivorous plants.

Sundews, pitcher plants and bladderworts are amazing thrivers in nutrient poor soils such as found in the Okefenokee Swamp. They have unique strategies for extracting essential nutrients from insects.

Sticky droplets on the ends of stalks erupting from the sundew's leaf pads trap flying and crawling insects. The

Lily Pad Lined Trail through Maul Hammock Lake

leaf pads slowly fold up to engulf their prey, digesting them with enzymes also on the leaf pads.

Pitcher plants lure insects with their irresistible scent. The scent is located at the lip of their elongated leaf that adapted into a long slender vase. A soup of digestive enzymes pools at the base of the slender leaf vase. Hair-like projections pointing downward towards the enzyme soup prevent the insect from escaping. Hapless unwary insects lured by a sweet scent are doomed to their imminent death.

Bladderworts are no less devious. Tiny little bladders that serve as adorable diminutive floats are also deadly. They too contain digestive enzymes. When a teeny tiny aquatic insect touches the bladder's hair-like trigger, the bladder implodes sucking in the helpless prey. All these carnivorous plants employ different but very clever strategies that help them thrive in nutrient poor soil.

In a mile or so we stopped to admire the grass pinks and rose pogonias (aka snakemouth orchids), lovely delicate ballet-pink and rose-colored ground orchids lining the trail. Soon Sam, Michelle, Linda, and Bob caught up with us. Crawfish immediately launched into interpretive hyper-drive. His spewed information pent up for far too long, pointing out all the details of these delicate pink beauties. His captive audience received and very much appreciated his fount of knowledge. He pointed out the honey guides and how insects can detect their ultraviolet beacons.

I added that sophisticated orchids, the most recent flowering plants to emerge on the evolutionary landscape, employ pollen-stamping mechanisms specific to their pollinators' morphology. More physiology. When a bee, mostly, lands on a petal guided by that ultraviolet honey guide, the leaf bends under the weight and another overhanging petal stamps the pollen on the bee's back. Another very clever design.

For the rest of the day we stopped every two or so miles to catch up and chat and impart natural history information. It was a grand day of delightful, easy paddling.

Michelle and Sam rekindled their father-daughter bond. Bob and Linda caught up on their respective busy lives and happily planned another getaway in a few months. Crawfish and I genuinely enjoyed each other's company. We didn't often have that opportunity anymore. We led trips with other less experienced co-leaders now, and were not at home at the same time much. That is hard on a marriage.

Eventually we transitioned from the broad expanse of green Sapling Prairie dotted with Sandhill Cranes and Great Blue Herons and Red-shouldered Hawks. Just after Dinner Pond we made our way through thick batteries, overhangs lined with hurrah bush, titi, sweetspire, and tangles of greenbriar. Tight turns and narrow passages tested our paddling skills.

Big Water Sign

Eventually our narrow canoe trail became officially named on our map as the famous Suwannee River. The river, made famous by Stephen C. Foster's song of the same name, flows out of the southwestern corner of the Okefenokee all the way to Gulf of Mexico mostly through Florida to her upper west coast. Famously, Stephen never saw the river. He just looked on a map for river names and the multi syllabic Suwannee fit his score.

A few miles further, we entered the incredible cathedral of Big Water. Towering a hundred feet above our heads, the feathery canopies of the majestic cypress with their broad sturdy buttressed trunks welcomed us. The Swamp's mood changed from bright, cheery, and open in the prairie to dark, moody, and mysterious beneath the statuesque feather-needled cypress.

The black mirrored water perfectly reflected the sky, cypress, us, everything. It picked up speed, and we barely wet our paddles. The canoes coasted down the waterway on their own, on a "Magical Mystery Tour" of this Great Swamp.

Around 4:00 PM we landed at the VIP cabin in Big Water. Quiet, hidden, cozy and rustic, it smelled of new paint. I guessed that John had dispatched a work crew to gussie up the place for our VIP as soon as he found out that Sam wanted to paddle. All of us do that. When company is coming, we go into hyper sprucing up mode.

Bob and Linda planned and packed the food, and they graciously, hospitably set out hors d'oeuvres for us to enjoy while Sam and Michelle asked questions about the dark water, cypress trees, orchids, Sandhill Cranes, owls, gators, otters, etc. Bob kept the wine poured while Linda offered cheese and crackers and grapes. Evening enveloped us. Crawfish glowed, finally allowed to give out all of that information pent up for far too long in his head.

Bob pulled out three cigars keeping one for himself and handed one to Sam and another to Crawfish. None offered to the ladies in company. So I rummaged around in my day pack and pulled out my own white metal tube encasing an old Portofino Macanudo from last summer's turtle nesting activities. Sam and Bob tried not to look shocked. Crawfish beamed.

Bugs can drive you crazy. No-see-ums in particular (sand gnats, biting midges) are the bane of sea turtle nesting observers. A long time ago someone suggested I find a good cigar to puff on, so on windless nights the smoke would repel the very pesky no-see-ums. I tried many a cigar and finally settled on the Portofino Macanudo. A bit pricey for a young naturalist, but being comfortable in no-see-um hell was well worth the seven or eight bucks for one cigar. Being ever frugal out of necessity, I discovered that you could fire one up, puff on it for several minutes, create a good cloud of bug-repelling smoke, snuff it out, stow it in its metal tube, and relight it many times before the taste became intolerable.

I didn't share any of this information and Crawfish didn't either. He especially reveled in the shock value of me puffing on that classy stogy.

And puff we did, for quite a while, on that screened-in porch, enjoying only good old normal small talk. "No politicking allowed," Sam ordered.

Bob and Linda eventually ghosted away to prepare dinner, previously prepped and frozen at home. It had been thawing throughout the day in a cooler and took only a few minutes to ready. I offered to help, but Bob and Linda had it completely under control. Grateful for a few moments to puff and sit and chew the fat with Sam and Michelle and Crawfish, I offered to wash dishes afterwards.

We savored incredibly delicious beef bourguignon over egg noodles. I couldn't believe the tenderness of the beef tips. The red wine paired perfectly with the thick, bursting-with-flavor rich sauce of the bourguignon. It melted in our mouths. I almost licked my plate, but Crawfish, knowing a few of the bad table habits taught me by my barbaric, fun-loving Hungarian father, gave me "the look", and I stopped before I started.

With dinner barely settled, Sam surprised the heck out of us by asking if we would take him and Michelle out in the canoes to shine gator eyes.

Crawfish and I exchanged shocked looks and said in unison, "Of course!" We loved shining gator eyes, and even though Refuge rules prohibited paddling at night, we figured Senator Sam had special permission.

We eagerly jumped into our canoes, and, as soon as we hit Big Water, on one of the darkest most overcast nights I can ever remember spending in the Swamp, Crawfish and I shone our headlamps all around, jack-lighting hundreds of pairs of red eyes. Quite spectacular, really. Crawfish studied alligators most of his career, and, since marrying him, I tagged along. After a few tagging forays, I learned I could handle up to a four-footer, maybe a subdued five-footer. Any gator larger than that called for the big boys. When tagging alligators and data collecting, it is very important to go with really big, strong people, at least for me anyway.

Alligators, like all nocturnal hunters, have a layer behind their retina that reflects light referred to as the tapetum lucidum. Light passing through the pupil onto the retina excites rods located there. Reflected by the tapetum lucidum the light passes back through the retina and stimulates the rods a second time. That

Big Water

adaptation enables nocturnal animals to see very well in the dark.

Humans don't have this layer. We are diurnal creatures with retinas loaded up with way more cones than rods. So we are more suited for daytime hunting and functioning. Those scary amber eyes in flash photos of yore resulted from dilated pupils that reflected the flash off the backs of our eyeballs that are densely populated with bright red blood vessels. The pre-flash in today's cameras constricts the pupil ahead of the actual flash that lights the photo, thus reducing the creepy red-eye phenomenon.

I love taking my guests on night hikes just to shine whatever eyes are out there. Raccoon eyes shine gold as do frog eyes. Hunting spiders shine luminescent green. (Web weaving spiders have reduced eye function since

214

Crawfish with 4' Gator - Shinin' Gator Eyes

they detect their prey by sensing vibrations on their
webs.) Moths, pink. Chuck-wills-widows, blood red.
Gators and crocs are red, but really more rosy red.

Teaching people how to shine eyes is easiest with
hunting spiders. And they are everywhere. With a
flashlight per person, I instruct my night prowlers to
hold their light up to their forehead with the beam
shining away like a miner's headlamp. This is important.
Once I actually had an adult complain he couldn't find
any eyes. When I turned around to help him, I really
had to control myself not to laugh out loud. He had the
lighted end held against his forehead. Even the kids
knew better than that.

Anyway, look down the light beam into the grass
or under the bushes or around the base of a house
or building. When you see a little bright green light
reflecting back at you, keep the green light in your
beam and follow it down to the source. Most likely you
will find a surprisingly small hunting spider whose
eyes you are illuminating. This is a very cool activity.
Kids love it. Old kids too.

On one occasion I saw many tiny bright luminescent green eyes shining back at me and couldn't figure out what I was seeing until I followed the beam down to the source. There in my spotlight basked a large mother wolf spider with her numerous spiderlings clinging to her back. Each one of those wee spiderling eyes illuminated just like Mom's. They sparkled and twinkled like the spectacular precious emerald-like jewels they were, center stage in my little spotlight.

Bob had one more issue to bend Sam's ear about. With the change in scenery, the politicking-free zone of the porch became null and void. So Crawfish and I drifted off with the current, treating ourselves to the highest concentration of gator eyes I think I had ever seen. Rose-red eyes shone everywhere. Big ones, little ones, in between ones popped up in every direction. Stunningly spectacular!

Eventually Sam and Bob resolved the issue, or at least Sam tired of the conversation and yelled out, "Hey Crawfish and Cathy, where are y'all?"

"Down this way!" I shone my light on myself, so they could orient in the darkness without losing too much night vision.

"Okay, gotcha! On our way!"

We heard Sam and Michelle's paddles tap their gunnels as they maneuvered their canoe to make way toward us. We heard them giving each other instruction. Their voices increased in volume, and then we heard a lot of shuffling sounds.

Then an almost inaudible plop. Swishing sounds. Water swirling.

Then a disquieting "Woohoo! Woohoo!"

Next, a hysterical "Oh My God! Oh My God! Sam and Michelle just capsized!"

Night Visitor (Photo by Todd Mussman)

Bob yelled out to us while Linda tried to keep their canoe upright in spite of her panicking husband's uncontrolled erratic movements.

"What?! Oh My God!" Crawfish boomed. "Atchy, shine the light on them! I'll paddle."

I did as directed. Crawfish put full muscle to paddle, nearly catapulting me out of the bow. Our canoe rocketed through the black waters of Big Water, leaving an impressive QEII wake behind. In a flash Crawfish blasted us onto the scene, nearly capsizing Linda and Bob with his turbo-speed wake.

There, calmly chatting as if nothing out of the ordinary, Michelle and Sam treaded water while clinging to their upended canoe. You'd have thought they were at Tybee Island on a warm summer's day, holding on to an inner tube while enjoying bobbing up and down in the warm ocean waves.

Bob and Linda reached them first and stood by to await instructions. The professionals needed to take charge of the scene. And Crawfish did.

In hyper-drive rescue mode, without even letting anyone know his intentions, not even me, Crawfish effortlessly scooped up feather-light Michelle out of the water and into our canoe with one hand. Caught a bit off guard I worked to stabilize our canoe but managed the task admirably I thought, on such spontaneous notice.

Michelle now in the middle of our canoe, on the bottom, shook out of fright and cold and wetness. I took off my jacket and put it around her.

Crawfish now barked out orders. As he did, he pulled our canoe alongside Bob and Linda's to transfer Michelle into it. We wanted their canoe on the other side of our canoe to stabilize us as we prepared to rescue Sam.

Sam weighed considerably more than Michelle and would certainly tip the canoe with the added weight of his now-soaked blue jeans and blue jean jacket.

Clothes made of denim are the worst to wear in watery environments. When wet they offer no insulation and are instead heat-wicking agents. They soak up and hold water. They make an immersed person immeasurably harder to rescue. Quick-dry synthetic materials are far superior.

This time Crawfish reviewed his rescue plan. He decided he would grab Sam by the belt and simply pull him into the middle of our canoe. Bob, Linda, Michelle and I would do our best to counter balance the canoe as Crawfish brought Sam's added weight and water into our canoe. Easy peasy, right?

"Everyone ready?" We all nodded and said yes nearly in unison. "Good. Okay, Sam, its show time. Here we go!"

Sam heaved his shoulders and arms over the gunnel and hung on to the side of the canoe waiting for the assist. Crawfish reached over him to grab his belt and pulled.

Bob, Linda and Michelle leaned away from Sam. I had a vice-like grip on their canoe. Crawfish's initial hard pull resulted in Sam rising up but not high enough to clear the gunnel. I really thought Crawfish might go in head first with his effort.

Linda, Michelle and Bob leaned farther to the opposite side to add more counter balance. I still had a death grip on Bob and Linda's canoe and watched in horror thinking this wouldn't end well. Michelle's eye were saucers. To her credit though she kept her weight low and smack dab in the center as instructed.

Crawfish eased Sam back down into the water. His

My Right Profile Is My Best

weight, much heavier with soaked jeans and jacket, proved too much even for Crawfish's herculean strength.

Crawfish reassessed the situation and told Sam he would count to three. On three he would pull him up, and, when that happened, Sam needed to kick his feet hard to help propel himself upward. Sam acknowledged.

We all readied ourselves to do our part in this dark-of-night, alligator-audience, Big Water, Okefenokee VIP rescue.

"Okay, let's try this again. Ready, Sam?"

"As ready as I'll ever be!"

"Okay, here we go. One, two, three!"

On three Crawfish put all of his massive muscles into his pull and reflexively grunted with the effort in a karate-like kiai.

Sam kicked his feet hard, frothing up the dark water like a whirling egg beater.

In a very noisy, yet remarkably coordinated maneuver, Sam's hips reached just enough height to breach the gunnel. Crawfish fell back into his seat as the bulk of Sam's weight broke free of the water's nearly firm hold. Exhausted by the effort, Sam struggled to get his legs over the gunnel. He kicked them high into the air, and a gush of water flooded over him into the canoe. Crawfish grabbed his flailing legs easing them into the canoe. Sam lay on the canoe bottom, now half full of water.

We all laughed in the sheer relief of a rescue successfully completed.

I am so very glad no cameras recorded this event.... for Sam's sake! Today had a cell phone video been rolling, this no doubt would have ended up going viral on YouTube.

Sam rested like a giant Pacific-coast fluke just landed into a catch boat. No flopping though. The cold water and fright knocked the shake and flop out of him.

As our relieved laughing subsided, we settled down and paddled back to the VIP cabin so Sam and Michelle could change clothes. Those extra pieces I packed came in handy. Michelle gladly accepted my extras. Bob, about Sam's size, shared some of his. Both Sam and Michelle could have easily fit, together, into any of Crawfish's. He is a big man, not overweight, just big.

While Sam and Michelle dried off and Bob and Linda tended them, Crawfish, still a bit damp, and I headed back out to retrieve the upturned canoe. It took only a few minutes to locate it. We emptied it by pulling it slowly upside down across our gunnels until it drained of nearly all the water. Then we righted it and tied it to our stern and towed it back to the cabin.

Rainbow Snake

The rest of that night tall tales spun round and round, and laughter rang out across the otherwise quietude of Big Water. Seems that when you share a life-threatening event together, all the walls of social protocol break down, at least for a short time anyway. It was a glorious night. A most memorable night.

The cast included the US Senator, the Executive Director of Georgia Conservancy, the College Co-Ed, the Distinguished Atlanta Attorney, and the Naturalists.

But this night we were all just Good Ole Swamp Buddies sharing a lot of tall tales. We certainly had knitted a new exciting yarn together.

Much later that night as I drifted off to sleep, I whispered to Crawfish what a different story this would have been if the headlines in tomorrow's newspapers read "Senator Sam Nunn Lost in Alligator Attack in Okefenokee Swamp."

My mind wandered further with the lead paragraph of the article.

"US Senator Sam Nunn, on track to be the next US President, drowned last night in an alligator attack.

Two reportedly "professional naturalists" entrusted with escorting his VIP party through the Okefenokee were unable to save the Senator and his college-aged daughter when their canoe tipped. The alligators, whose eyes they were illegally shining, attacked immediately. Mercifully for the Senator and his daughter their end came quickly. Charges against the naturalists who ironically survived have not yet been filed."

Oh, what a night!

*P*ostscript:

The most frequently asked questions by people on their first adventure into the Swamp are "Will I be eaten by an alligator if I fall in the water?" and "Will a snake drop off a branch into my canoe?"

On the over 300 overnight trips I have been privileged to lead into the Swamp as of this story's writing, I have never had a snake drop into my canoe. I have seen them

Don't Feed Alligators Sign

223

sunning on branches overhanging the canoe trails. However none have actually fallen into my canoe....yet.

On all those many overnight and day trips through the Okefenokee, I have only had to fish six people out of the water. All tipped their canoes during the alligators' feeding season, and not one gator moved a muscle towards the immersed humans.

Not even the horrifying time when a father and his small daughter flipped. Not one alligator even so much as looked their way. Having a small child go in had always been my worst nightmare. I figured a small human body would be easy pickings for a large alligator. Not so this time anyway. I am sure the loud splash and noises we made repelled, not attracted, even the hungriest gator.

Oddly the father, with his daughter safely in the middle of my very upright canoe, ordered me to dive to the bottom of Billy's Lake to retrieve his money belt. Really, you put your money belt in the bottom of your canoe? Nope, no can do.

Outdoor Rule #1: In a boat, all irreplaceable items should be waterproofed.

Never take anything in a canoe or boat unless it is placed in a sealed waterproof container or unless you don't mind losing it should you tip, and that most certainly includes a money belt full of money.

Outdoor Rule #2: Never feed a wild animal.

Alligator attacks typically occur where alligators are used to being fed by humans. Gators, like other wild animals fed by humans, lose their fear of us and therefore expect food from all humans by association. When it is not delivered, usually the conditioned alligator or other wild animal aggressively approaches the human for the expected hand out. Then the gator or bear or raccoon, or any other human-fed wild animal must be destroyed to prevent future attacks.

Outdoor Rule #2 Exception: Bird feeding stations are sanctioned and encouraged as long as the bird seeds and suet, and for hummingbirds sugar water of the correct proportions, are managed, cleaned and changed frequently and placed in a location safe from predators especially cats.

Outdoor Rule #3: Do not swim in areas posted "NO SWIMMING."

The second-most typical scenario for an alligator attack is when a human is swimming in a clearly posted area marked "NO SWIMMING". Alligators size us and other animals up horizontally and vertically. A horizontal profile presented to a large gator is fair game. A vertical profile presented to an alligator whose entire orientation is horizontal is much more intimidating. Signs are posted by authorities for a reason. The reason for "no swimming" most likely is that a large alligator resides in the area.

Outdoor Rule #4: Don't walk your dog or any small

Gator Comfort

pet around a pond where alligators reside and for heaven's sake, don't let your dog bark near a gator pond.

 The third-most typical scenario for a negative alligator-human interaction is when a pet owner walks their dog too close to a gator pond. The bark of a dog is just the right frequency and basically music to an alligator's ear, the music of a dinner bell that is. Usually the owner tries to save their dog, but the very ancient, instinctually determined alligator latches onto its prey and pulls it under water to drown it. That's how it's done. If the human doesn't let go, the human goes too. Unfortunately this happens.

 Alligators drown their prey and if too large to consume whole on the spot, they stuff their prey under a submerged log or bank undercut to let it season. After a few days the meat is tender enough for the alligator to pull and twist off chunks.

*P*ost, *Postscript:*

 All bodies of water and waterways in the Southeast have, will have, or have had an alligator or several residing in them. It's a given.

CHAPTER 9

Wind Fever

Round Top

Spring 1982

At Wilderness Southeast company policy is two leaders on each trip. Safety first and foremost, safety always. With two leaders, if an emergency occurred, and it rarely did, one leader could tend to the injured or ill, and the other could still carry on with the trip. The policy makes sense. We always had two leaders on each trip....until the spring of 1982.

We were so busy packing food and gear for as many as five trips in the field at one time, all of us were working triple overtime. Even our office staff were pressed into service as co-leaders and in some cases as cooks for the really large school groups. No surprise then that one regularly scheduled advertised Okefenokee Swamp trip had been overlooked. It had literally dropped through the proverbial cracks of administrative attention.

Apparently a few cancellations occurred months before the start date of this particular trip. No problem. Spring Okefenokee trips always filled. No doubt others would reserve prior to the start date. No worries. But they didn't, and no one caught the anomaly.

Three days before the start of the trip, Bruce, our Program Director, called to ask if I would consider leading the trip by myself. With only three people signed up, it really didn't make sense to send two leaders since it was just an overnight trip anyway and we really didn't want to cancel the trip at this late date.

So that is how I came to "take one" for the company. Against my better judgement, I agreed to lead the trip. What could possibly go wrong on an overnighter?

The three guests were a mother, Jeannie, her 12-year-old son Randy, and Kelly, a single lady about my age.

This would become the most memorable trip I would ever have in the Okefenokee Swamp, and I have led plenty of trips into the hallowed place. When parents register their children on regularly scheduled trips, on which most participants are adults, the parent is responsible for paddling with their child. That is another hard, fast rule. It is unfair to expect a trip leader to paddle a child when leaders need to tend to everyone in the group. If as a leader you are paddling and tending to a child in your canoe, it is hard to pay attention to the rest of the group.

I asked Bruce if Jeannie understood and agreed to this rule. She did. Okay then, I could do this.

I picked up Kelly at her Bed & Breakfast on West Gaston Street in Savannah at 6:30AM. I never liked getting up early. I just didn't like hearing the harsh stab of an alarm clock assaulting my slumbering ears. Since I had to get myself up and drive to our headquarters to get the van that had been loaded with gear and food and hitch up the canoe trailer, I had to get up way too early. I much prefer to wake up naturally with the sun. After all I am a naturalist.

Kelly giddily bounced out of the B&B's door with her gear in hand. I ran up the stairs to help her, but she had it under control. I already liked this woman. Anyone who can be that cheerful this early in the morning, and before her first cup of coffee I soon discovered, would be a pleasure to be around.

Kelly looked as perky as her personality. Her short dark hair perfectly framed her lightly freckled cheeks that bunched up into pleasing round pinkish knolls when she smiled. And she mostly smiled. About my height and build, we would be perfectly matched canoe partners. Her pale skin signaled a Scotch-Irish heritage, so I made note to make sure she slathered up every day. Actually that had become a mantra of mine anyway. "Put on sunscreen before you put on your clothes. Use the buddy system to cover those hard-to-reach places. See who can give the other the best early morning rub down." Well, you had to make it interesting to adults.

My other two guests were to meet us at Suwannee Canal Recreation Area (SCRA) parking lot at 9:00AM. Kelly and I had plenty of time to swing by Ronnie's on our way out of town to grab breakfast. I loved Ronnie's milkshakes, but an early morning sugar high would only result in an energy-sapping crash 15 minutes later. I opted for an egg and sausage biscuit and unsweetened ice tea. Switching from sweetened tea to unsweetened was the hardest dietary change I had to make when I became aware of my hypoglycemia. After a while though sweet tea tasted so sickly sweet I just couldn't abide it anymore. Good thing.

Kelly and I chatted easily all the way down I-95 and then across smaller highways to Folkston. We arrived at SCRA just before 9:00AM. I picked out Jeannie and

Beautiful Day in the Okefenokee

Randy right away as they crossed the parking lot with all the other visitors.

Jeannie, stunningly beautiful with shoulder length softly curled blond hair and striking blue eyes, still had a Barbie doll figure. I thought, "Wow, a potential beauty queen." Turns out she had been. After winning the Miss Georgia title in the mid-1960's, she went on to become runner-up to Miss America. All smiles, she shook my hand. I noticed it shook a bit though. Reaching for her son's shoulder, she pulled him in close, and introduced him as Randy.

"This is Randy's 12th birthday, and this trip is his special birthday request."

Mother and son exchanged big loving smiles. Kelly and I too smiled at this lovely display of family harmony and domestic bliss.

I let that mellow scene linger a few seconds and then wasted no time in launching into packing the canoes. I ordered my three charges to bring certain items in certain order. While doing this I intermittently sized up the paddling experience of Jeannie and Randy. From our two hours of conversation as we drove down to the Swamp, I knew that Kelly had paddled quite a bit.

"So, how much have you paddled, Jeannie?"

"Oh, I just love to paddle!"

"Uh huh, and just how much has that been?"

"Oh, well, you know, I used to paddle quite a bit."

"Yes, well, and just how long ago was that?"

"Well, let's see, it's been a few years now. I paddled a lot at Camp Chewonkee."

"Oh, were you a camp counselor?"

"No, when I attended camp."

"Uh huh, recently?" I couldn't imagine an adult camp, but strange things are out there. I started to fret about where this twenty-questions dialog was heading. "Well, no, I camped as a camper....when I was ten." She looked away as she let those last words string from her mouth.

"Ten?!?!" I screamed in my head. "Egad!" What came

out of my mouth however had been tempered by seasons of dealing with the unexpected on these trips.

"So, it's been a while since you've paddled, but you think you can handle paddling Randy?"

"Oh yes, Gussie who helped me make reservations in your office made it perfectly clear I would have to paddle with Randy, or otherwise we couldn't go on this trip."

Jeannie smiled sweetly with those big full lips and enormous azure blue eyes.

I smiled back with my thin lips pursed and my hazel-brown eyes skeptically narrowed. I just didn't think this would go as planned.

When Randy brought an armload of tents to the canoe staging area, I engaged him in conversation while his mother returned to her car for more personal gear.

"So, Randy, have you paddled before, or is this your first time in a canoe?"

"Oh no, Ma'am! I have been practicing in our pool. A friend of my mother's has a canoe, and he brought it over so I could practice paddling."

"Well, how nice. So you and your mom have been paddling back and forth in your pool?"

"Yes, Ma'am. Well, I have anyway. Almost every day after school for a half hour or so and on weekends for a little longer."

I rolled my eyes. Oh man, this was not going to go well.

I sighed deeply and reflexively rolled my shoulders in preparation for the paddle.

When I finished packing both canoes, Kelly settled herself into the bow of our perfectly trimmed canoe.

Paddling Down Suwannee Canal

Our body weights of about 125 were perfectly matched.
Her arms looked a bit thin, but that didn't matter.
Mine were well-toned from many paddling adventures.
All she need do was keep her paddle wet and keep us
moving forward. Before launching our canoe, I helped
Randy into the bow of his and then his mother into her
stern seat. When she grabbed the paddle incorrectly, I
gave her quick instructions on how to hold the paddle
and how to use it. I did the same with Randy. He was
giddy and very ready for this adventure. In contrast
Jeannie frowned and moved nervously in her seat. Her

233

hands shook a bit as I showed her the proper way to grasp the paddle. Then she air paddled as I gave instructions on how to actually paddle.

"Are you both okay and ready for this grand adventure?" I asked as jauntily as I could.

"Yes! Yes! Yes!" Randy exclaimed at the top of his lungs.

"I guess," Jeannie said tentatively as she bit her naturally puffy bottom lip.

Shoving them off took a bit of effort since they were really too far up on land. Jeannie didn't want to get her feet wet, so she entered the canoe before I had time to push Randy out a bit further on to the water. Though still trim with her Barbie doll figure, she had Kelly and me by many pounds. The gear and food in the canoe added to the heft and I grunted as I pushed.

Jeannie actually screamed slightly as the canoe broke free of the sand's friction. The canoe bobbled as its weight equilibrated in the water. And they were off!

I leaned over the stern of my canoe, gripping the gunnels with both hands, and placed one foot on the bottom. With the other foot still on the sand bank I pushed off. We easily glided off the bank bobbling on to the water. Now we were off!

Jeannie stoically, bravely paddled for almost two miles, zigzagging down the Suwannee Canal. Randy, having the time of his young life, thought this was normal progress and delighted each time they brushed the shrubs on opposite sides of the canal.

I knew that it would go exactly like this. Jeannie would struggle to keep their canoe on course. Randy wouldn't know the difference. In his sheltered kid world all was right and good. Jeannie in her mother world was making great sacrifices. Just how great a sacrifice, I wouldn't know until months later.

I let the farce of Jeannie's paddling expertise go on for a mile and a half. Some part of me wanted her to learn a lesson. Never over state your skills, especially when you are going to impact the experience of others.

"Kelly, this is not going well. Do you think you could paddle with Jeannie? She seems to be strong enough, but she doesn't have the skills to steer her canoe. If she keeps up this pace, we won't get to Round Top until midnight."

"Yes, of course! I wondered when you were going to pull the plug. I'll be happy to paddle with her."

I told Randy I wanted to paddle with him in my bow. I had a lot of things I wanted to show him in honor of his 12th birthday, a very special birthday indeed. He jumped at the chance, but then the very thoughtful young man turned to his mother and asked her if she would be okay with that.

Jeannie said she thought that is exactly what he should do and smiled at me gratefully.

For the rest of the nine miles down the canal and the last three miles through Grand Prairie to Round Top, Randy and I laughed and chatted and had a rollicking good time. He asked about frogs in particular, so we stopped in the prairie to observe tiny cricket frogs hopping from lily pad to lily pad. When one jumped onto the side of the canoe close to his seat, he shrieked in delight. He motioned excitedly for his mother to pull alongside to see. Jeannie dutifully oohed and aahed at the tiny little brown fellow with a faint yellow Y marking on his back. Two yellow lines streaking from his eyes joined to form the pedestal of the Y down his little bumpy back. She pulled out her camera to snap a few memories.

As instructed, Randy gently moved a finger behind

the frog while holding his other cupped hand in front of it. The tactic worked. The frog perched for just a moment on his finger. Randy, absolutely thrilled, brought it close to his face for closer inspection. The frog, much to Randy's surprise, leapt from his finger to the side of his face. Randy instinctively froze and shifted his eyes downward to view his new cheek ornament. His mother's camera clicked off a few quick shots. Those no doubt still hold a place in one of the family's cherished photo albums.

We talked about water striders and water spiders and how tufts on the ends of their feet distribute their weight. So well in fact that they do not break through the surface tension of the weak hydrogen bonds of the water. I instructed him to observe the feet where they touched the water to see how the water's surface tension barely held up against their diminutive weight. Their feet literally made small depressions in the water's surface. They looked as if they walked on a watery trampoline.

"Fascinating".

If I hadn't been looking at him, I would have sworn the utterance had come from Mr. Spock himself. Instead it issued from my twelve year old charge. I wasn't sure if he understood the physics, but he seemed to take it all in.

As an added challenge, I directed him to observe the tip end of his paddle every time it came out of the water. He did.

I explained that the droplets of water formed perfect spheres as a result of gravity and centrifugal force on their short fall from paddle tip to water's surface. The droplets had enough cohesion to stay together as spheres for a second or two. Then the hydrogen bonds in the droplet would weaken and recombine with those on the surface.

Water Clouds

The droplets then disappeared into the matrix of the dark Swamp water.

Randy sat transfixed. He peered intently at the droplets, closely watching each one hit the water and skitter across the surface before being absorbed into the matrix.

This kid impressed me to the max. Polite, respectful, interested, caring, thoughtful, happy. As we say in the South, his parents had "raised him right."

By the time we rounded the corner to make the last mile-and-a-half push to Round Top, the wind picked up. It had been blowing a steady breeze all day long, mostly at our backs. Had we been paddling into it, we would have experienced a different paddling adventure. It would have been much harder and more painful. Thankfully, we sailed to our platform with ease.

Kelly looked a bit tired, but her good humor and good spirits lifted Jeannie's sagging ones. Jeannie felt she had let her son down by not paddling with him. He didn't seem to mind though since he got to be with me. Actually he really enjoyed the total natural history immersion with me.

Kelly and Jeannie chatted amiably, and Kelly learned

a lot about Jeannie. It seemed Jeannie needed to spill, and spill she did. She shared that she was enduring a horrible, devastating, humiliating divorce. Jeannie had lived a dream life in a dream house with her rich plastic surgeon husband for nearly two decades. They successfully raised their daughter into a respectful teenager who asserted independence in an acceptable manner and then Randy. And you know how I felt about Randy.

A few months prior to this trip however, Jeannie's perfect dream world began to unravel. She first noticed charges on the joint credit card account for expensive jewelry she had not purchased nor received as gifts from husband. Then she noticed hotel expenses from his conference trips that didn't make sense either. Charges for beauty salon, day spa, nail salon. Jim wouldn't use those services.

Eventually Jeannie had to face the obvious.

When she confronted her husband, he of course denied her allegations. But he couldn't explain them

Never Wet or Golden Club

away either. The final confrontation came when
Jim said he would be coming home late because an
unexpected meeting had been called by the hospital
administrator. That didn't happen often, but it did
happen.

Jeannie decided to check up on her husband. As soon
as she hung up, she made her way to the hospital
in her Mercedes. She arrived just in time to see her
husband of nineteen years with his arm around a very
young pretty nurse walking to his Mercedes. Jeannie
crumpled onto the steering wheel, setting off a long
loud blast.

Jim and his sweet young thing instinctively looked
over at the car. Like everyone else in the parking lot.
Jim dutifully helped his date into his Mercedes and
then went to Jeannie's.

"Really, Jeannie? Do you want the entire hospital to
see what you're doing?"

"Me? You giant stinking asshole! You're the one
who's the problem here!"

Beauty queens, even in time of duress, use relatively
polite epithets.

As soon as Jeannie returned home, she called family friend
and lawyer Richard. She wanted a divorce immediately.
Richard of course needed more information but not
much more. He had known for quite a while. How
could Jeannie not have known? When you don't want
to know, you don't. It's as simple as that.

Kelly filled me in on all of this later, on our drive
home. I knew none of it while in the Swamp. It
wouldn't have made a difference anyway. The rest of
the trip unfolded regardless and in spite of our human
frailties and shortcomings.

At long last I spotted the twirling air turbine on top

of the chemical toilet of Round Top platform. It's amazing how something as unnatural to this very natural setting as this twirling metal contraption can bring such a wash of relief over tired aching shoulder muscles. I maneuvered our canoe alongside the platform.

Randy had stopped paddling miles back when we stopped to look at frogs and water striders and spiders. I knew he was tired, so I let him look and explore without paddling. Besides, the wind pushed us along nicely, and I didn't really need his help. Just seeing the joy of discovery rewarded me for my extra efforts.

As we began unloading the canoes, we had the first indication that the wind might cause some trouble when a life preserver took to the air in an amazing display of aerobatics. The wind whistled through the struts of the platform and lifted the very light-weight yolk-style garish orange PFD into flight from its resting place. No matter, an outstretched reach with the grip-end of the paddle retrieved it quickly enough. Randy busied himself making sure nothing else took flight.

With everything out of the canoes I made sure to

10' Gator in Suwannee Canal Basin

secure the painters with an extra line. I didn't want to swim after our canoes should the wind increase and they loosen up and go on a sail-about by themselves.

Now that we were no longer running with the wind but were now standing against it, it became apparent to me it had increased considerably. Jeannie tensed up. At my insistence she sat down to catch her breath, but that seemed to only heighten her state of agitation. Randy, bless his little soul, helped Kelly, bless her big soul, and I set up our tents for the night. With only four of us, I felt justified in packing separate tents for me and Kelly. No need to double up if you don't have to in those cramped little Hirsch Weiss tents.

With the wind whipping around the platform struts and picking up anything not secured, we nearly lost Randy as he held the body of the first tent we were attempting to set up. He clung onto the flapping nylon for dear life. It nearly lifted him up a few times until I yelled for him to drop it to the floor and step on it. He did. Whew. I didn't need a kid going airborne over Grand Prairie. Jeannie sat nearly catatonic now. I couldn't get to her right away since I needed to set up our tents and get dinner going as my first priorities. Now the door to the chemical toilet began to bang wildly, and with each loud bang Jeannie jumped. It banged repeatedly over several minutes until I located a large skein of cord. I tied a bowline around the outside door handle and then moved around the structure, wrapping the line as tightly as I could. When I reached the door handle again, I tied a series of half hitches to secure it shut and also make it easy to release the line so we could use the facility.

With that loud disruptive noise abated for the moment anyway, I turned my attention back to pitching tents. Kelly, Randy, and I set the first one up with a lot of difficulty, but at least the three of us held on to it well enough. While Kelly and Randy held the first one in

241

place, I ran a long line through the eye rings where normally a tent stake would secure the tent floor to the ground. No ground here, so I tied the tent corners to the struts of the platform.

With that task accomplished, Randy and Kelly let go a bit prematurely. The tent billowed up like a mindless gray apparition. Tethered by my lines, it contorted in all kinds of interesting shapes and configurations. Randy, Kelly, and I were very amused by this billowing specter. We laughed and made comments.

"Wait, now it's a giant scorched morphing marshmallow!" Randy laughed.

"Yeah, okay, but now it's a, wait for it, wait for it, now, now it's a giant puffball mushroom spewing out reproductive spores!"

Kelly and Randy looked at me as if I had horns coming out of my head. Okay, I guess I put too much of my naturalist's interpretation in there and not enough of my creative silly side.

Kelly offered her take next. "Okay, okayyyyy, nowwwwww, it's the BLOB!!!!"

She grabbed up Randy and twirled him round and round. He squealed his surprised and gleeful delight.

I looked over at Jeannie to see if she too enjoyed the humor. Nope. She sat with a vacant look on her face. I didn't see this coming. Oh My!

I directed Kelly and Randy to put Jeannie and Randy's gear in the tent to hold it down. They did so with dispatch.

Next, the three of us quickly, expertly, pitched the remaining two tents, putting our respective gear in them to hold them down.

I suggested to Jeannie that she might want to lie

Tom, Cathy, Suzanna, George at Round Top (Photo by Frank Wooldridge)

down for a quick nap before dinner. She nodded in agreement, and Randy and I helped her into her tent. She told Randy to stay inside with her. She did not want to be alone, even though we were all right there just a few feet away with only a millimeter or two of cloth visually separating us from each other.

As unbelievable as it seemed to me, the wind howled now in a fresh breeze approaching 20 knots. Small trees – hollies, bays and magnolias – and shrubs bent in the wind and swayed back when it let up for a moment. They thrashed in the fiercely increasing wind.

I enlisted Kelly's help to put up tarps as windbreaks. They normally go under the tents to protect them from things that might rip them up from the ground. No such problem here. The tents were pitched, well sort of, on smooth boards of the platform floor. Now the tarps might help block the wind somewhat, or at least divert it enough for me to light a stove to cook dinner.

The platforms are about 30' by 20' with an additional section for the chemical toilet. They have a tin roof and open sides. When the wind blows, the platform offers

Okefenokee Idyll

little resistance. That is the only way they survive the fierce thunderstorms that build up and unleash their fury during the summer months.

Even in spring and fall, thunderstorms can build up. If you're still en route to your campsite, you might find yourself hunkered down in the bottom of your canoe to present as low of a profile as possible to the explosive bursts of wind. When there's a threat of lightning, you may find yourself huddled up in a fetal position, with only your feet touching the seat cushion that you have now placed in the bottom of your canoe to serve as insulation between you and any metal on the canoe or your gear. It can be a tough balancing act, especially in strong wind and especially with a full bladder.

The Okefenokee Swamp has her own microclimate. This vast expanse of watery landscape heats and cools at a different rate than surrounding areas, which are mostly arid pine forests. The most noticeable patterns occur in the summer months, but spring and fall have them as well. The black surface of the tannin darkened water absorbs heat while the green tree canopies are slower to heat up. A mixing of this warm and cooler air occurs, with the warm air rising and the cooler air staying put or falling. Eventually enough transfer evaporation occurs that the air above the Swamp becomes so heavy with moisture it has to unload.

An upward movement of hot air collides with the cooler upper heavily moisture-laden air. Then, Kaboom! All hell breaks loose. Thor unleashes his mighty wrath. Lightning bolts hurl with abandon on the leading edge of any system of the day or hour for that matter. It is quite a spectacular natural display of fireworks. If you are in the middle of it however, it is absolutely terrifying.

Some who have been with me over the years know that when I start singing I am in my most nervous state. I sing because it comforts me and because I hope it will comfort those who have entrusted their very lives to me. Most of the time it works. For those who have been through the drill before, my singing can have the opposite effect, alerting them to get even more nervous. So now I have to be judicious with my singing in times of duress. Oh well.

The wind freshened into a stiff breeze up to 27 knots.

Large cypress trees were bending to the wind and loose branches flew through the air.

The tarps that we put up as wind shields, billowed, retracted, snapped, and popped in the ever-increasing wind. They were breaking the wind for the most part, but I still struggled to keep a burner lit long enough just to make hot water. I figured a nice cup of hot chocolate would be just the comfort food this situation warranted. I asked Kelly to rouse Jeannie and Randy. Kelly reported back to me that Jeannie wanted to speak to me in person.

I turned off the stove, gave Kelly her cup and took two cups of steaming hot cocoa to Jeannie's tent.

Jeannie rocked back and forth with eyes as big as saucers. Randy held his mother's hand.

"Cathy, I just cannot do this. You're just going to have to call the ranger to come get us. We need to get out of here. This is bad. Really bad!"

"So, what's the problem Jeannie? Are you hurt or sick?"

"No, I just cannot move. My muscles are completely gone, and I just don't even feel like eating or unpacking or helping my baby boy, or....." Her voice trailed off as she put her hands to her face and began to sob. Randy hugged his mother. I sat the steaming cups outside the tent and unzipped the tent screen to hug her too. She shook uncontrollably.

"It's okay, it's okay, Jeannie. I know you're tired and this is all new to you and the wind is blowing and it's not the beautiful sunset you expected. I promise it'll get better. The wind is really the issue here. It makes everyone and everything jumpy."

"I don't care. I want to go home now!"

Red Trail Reflections

"I get that, Jeannie, but there's no way to call a ranger to come get us. There are no phone booths out here, and I don't have a CB radio with battery power. We are without communication to the outside world. We are on our own out here."

She did not want to hear this and looked at me and then howled.

Randy again comforted his mother. Nice kid.

"Look, there's really no use in getting so upset. Let's just calm down and think about getting a good rest tonight, so we can be fresh for paddling in the morning. I can't keep the stove lit for very long, so we'll just eat tomorrow's lunch. At lunch time tomorrow we'll be in a more sheltered place where I can cook tonight's dinner. Sound good?"

Randy eagerly nodded his head and looked to his mother who had no choice but to agree.

"Mom, you stay right here. I'll bring our dinner to you, and we'll have a little picnic right here in our tent."

I loved this kid!

I had wine for us adults but decided it would not be a good idea to uncork it. I would need all of my faculties sharp for the night. I didn't know what the night would bring, but whatever it brought, I wanted to be in full mental acuity.

The wind picked up to nearly gale force now - over 30 knots. We could barely move against it as we bustled about on the platform. Our clothes flapped so hard I thought they would flap right off!

The lines on the chemical toilet loosened and the door now banged abruptly in rapid succession. Kelly hopped to and secured it in no time. Each new noise added to Jeannie's heightening anxiety. She skidded down a dark, foreboding emotional tunnel to which I was not privy.

In the meantime Randy brought his mother and himself lunch-supper. Kelly and I sat outside their tent and yelled over the wind, trying to carry on a pleasant conversation extolling the wonderful sights and sounds of the day. Jeannie didn't participate.

As we sipped our now cold cocoa, Randy excitedly recounted each and every experience. He detailed the cricket frog jumping on to the side of his canoe and then how he got it up on his finger. He winked at me. He told Kelly about the water's surface tension and how the water striders and water spiders manage to skim across the surface without breaking through it. Then he expertly described how the weak hydrogen bonds of water droplets bead up as they drip from the tip of your paddle.

Did I mention I really loved this kid? Oh what a joy he was and I am sure still is!

There wasn't much use in trying to carry on any more activities for the night. A night paddle was out of consideration. The wind blew so hard now that small limbs and other plant parts hurled through the air hurting when they hit. I felt uncomfortable and knew Jeannie was just plain miserable. I put on my most cheerful face and tried to allay her fears. She seemed to be receptive, so I took that as a good sign.

Kelly and I talked for a bit longer, and then I announced I needed to lie down. Kelly did the same.

Randy, already my hero, continued to console his mother. I could hear his soft murmurs and imagined him gently patting and stroking his mother's soft blond curls to comfort her. He kept one hand up to keep the tent from touching her. The wind gusts pushed down on our little tent city and collapsed them momentarily. To their credit they sprang back up as the wind abated. Until the next big gust blew.

I don't know when I drifted off to sleep or how long I had been out when a branch, catapulted by the incessant and ever-increasing wind, blew up against one of the tarps. It hit the tarp with a loud thud and then ripped it dramatically loudly.

The wind had intensified to a full gale of 40 knots. It howled unmercifully. Everything on the platform rattled and shook. Including the platform. Including us.

The flapping tarps only added to the intensity and the ever-increasing anxiety of each of us and especially Jeannie. We were in a bad situation.

I got out of my convulsing tent to take down the tarps. They would end up ripped to shreds in this wind anyway. Kelly, bless her, got up to help.

As I returned to my even-more-convulsing tent, and while I waited for a break in the wind to enter my tent without having to fight it, I saw Jeannie silhouetted in her tent. She rocked back and forth, back and forth. Randy read to her by flashlight to soothe her anxiety. It didn't work. He too fought the tent to keep it off his mom.

"CATHY, CATHY! I INSIST. TAKE ME BACK NOW!"

"No, I can't do that Jeannie. It would be very unsafe for us to venture out now in our canoes in this howling wind in the dark. We are far better off to ride out the wind right here."

"MY TENT IS LIFTING OFF, AND RANDY AND I ARE GOING TO BE TRAPPED IN IT WHEN IT GOES INTO THE WATER. SO HOW CAN THAT BE SAFER THAN GOING HOME?"

"Ah ha, I see, well, as long as you and Randy stay in the tent, it isn't going to go anywhere and certainly not off the platform into the water."

"WE'RE GETTING INTO YOUR TENT WITH YOU."

No, that won't work. The tents are so small we'll be too crowded."

"WELL AT LEAST THERE'LL BE MORE WEIGHT IN THE TENT, AND IT WON'T BLOW OFF!"

"It's not going to blow off. I guarantee it. Please lie back down and try to sleep. You're going to need your energy for tomorrow."

"Mom, mom, don't worry. I have my knife right here in my hand. If our tent blows into the water, I'll cut us out of it."

This kid was a gem!

For a few hours more the wind stayed at a full gale gusting up to 50 to 60 knots at times. Seeds, seed heads, branches, and even a few large limbs crashed up against our tents, clanged on to the tin roof, and thickly littered the platform floor. It was a very intense night. The most intense night I have ever spent in the Swamp. I didn't like it. This strong wind really scared me. Most of the night our tents stayed flattened on top of us, leaving no headspace. The ties and aluminum poles just could not stand up against this kind of wind. These tents were designed to shed wind. Not this strong though.

Sometime around 4:00AM the wind died. I mean it just died completely. Not a wisp. I immediately fell into a deep sleep. Everyone else must have done so too. We slept the sleep of the dead tired because we were.

I have experienced this phenomenon in several different places along the southeast coast. A few hours before sunrise the wind dies completely. I have been caught once and only once by this.

On one Okefenokee trip with 18 guests the wind had been blowing steadily, pleasantly all day. Because many tents crowded the platform, I announced I would not pitch a tent this particular night. A few of

Calm-Before-the-Storm Sunrise at Round Top

my guests, trusting their intrepid leader, followed my lead, happy for the new found freedom of camping under the stars. At 4:00AM or thereabouts my tent-less guests, who previously had praised my name for giving them such spectacular front row seats to the stars, now cursed me. A cloud of mosquitoes descended on our unprotected faces and hands and any other exposed body parts. Thenceforth I never camped tent-less again.

Around 6:00AM I felt the first telltale flapping of my tent walls. I roused my charges and instructed them to pack up their gear and take down their tents. I quickly whipped up a hearty breakfast of hot water for coffee, tea, and cocoa while the low wind allowed for the flame to stay lit on my stove. I scrambled eggs in butter, fried lean bacon to a crisp, and browned several slices of toast in a dry frying pan.

We all wolfed it down, and I secretly wished for more. I cooked all I had packed, so I brought out leftover cookies from yesterday's lunch to finish off breakfast, not for me, but for Randy and Kelly.

As I busied myself with cleaning up the kitchen, packing it up in the proper boxes and coolers, Kelly and Randy took down the tents and packed them in stuff sacks. We were whirling dervishes of activity. All that is except Jeannie. She sat on the bench looking vacantly at her feet. I had no time to deal with her at the moment. My immediate objective was to get all of us in the canoes and down the trail and out of the prairie into the relative protective shelter of the Suwannee Canal before the wind might intensify again.

The wind picked up a bit more as we broke camp. Still Jeannie sat.

I assumed Jeannie would get her rear in gear eventually, but she didn't. So I finally sat down beside her for a chat.

"So, Jeannie, I know you aren't feeling that rested and you're not as confident about your abilities to paddle today. Am I right?"

She turned her head, and to my horror her beautiful azure-blue eyes had somehow turned a dark color, a possessed demonic dark color. Terror had overcome her.

"I AM NOT GETTING IN THAT CANOE. YOU ARE GOING TO HAVE TO CALL A RANGER TO COME GET ME!"

Jeannie yelled at the top of her lungs.

Last night she had yelled too, but I didn't notice the extent. The wind howled so loudly I thought she yelled to be heard over the noise. Her yelling indicated a much deeper problem.

Randy, startled, ran to his mother's side. In Jeannie's demonic state she pushed him away.

I looked to Kelly. Reading my mind, she grabbed Randy in a bear hug and ushered him off as far to the other side of the platform as she could, as far away from his mother as she could get him.

"Jeannie, you are going to have to calm down....."

"CALM DOWN? CALM DOWN? DO YOU KNOW WHAT I JUST WENT THROUGH LAST NIGHT???"

"Yes, Jeannie, I've been here the entire time. We all have. We have all experienced the wind and it's un......"

"I CANNOT DO THIS! I CANNOT DO THIS! THIS IS CRAZY! THIS IS INSANE!!!"

Jeannie's chest heaved in deep, quick, panicked breaths.

Not connecting with Jeannie, I remembered that, to get someone's attention who is yelling, you have to yell back at the same decibel level and then bring them down to a normal talking level. I didn't have any other options, so I gave it a try.

"JEANNIE, I CANNOT TALK TO YOU WHEN YOU ARE YELLING LIKE THIS!!! CAN WE AGREE NOT TO YELL?? WILL YOU Talk To Me In A Normal Voice? I would really like to hear what you have to say, but I can't because you are yelling at me."

Jeannie flinched as I punctuated each word I yelled. To my relieved surprise the method worked. Jeannie calmed down. With her breathing returning to nearly normal, I continued.

"You know, Jeannie, all in the world you're experiencing is wind fever. It's quite a well-known phenomenon. Sir Earnest Shackleton who explored Antarctica experienced it. He referred to it as malaise. Shackleton and his men nearly went crazy because of it."

I had just read the riveting account of the ordeal in the book Endurance written by the ship's Captain Frank A. Worsley and now employed my newly acquired knowledge on the subject of malaise or wind fever. Jeannie listened still looking at her feet.

"I've observed this often in animals too. When the wind blows hard, it moves branches, limbs, dirt, anything in its path. Noise accompanies the wind. Loud noises. It makes it difficult for the animals to sense where danger might come from next. So they're on edge. Their skin is pummeled by the wind, and every nerve in their body is on edge."

Jeannie perked up. She looked at me. Her eyes attentive to mine. I was connecting.

"I'm sure that's exactly what you're experiencing. You feel nauseous and like you've just gotta scream. Like you just can't take it anymore."

Now I read her every symptom. I told her exactly what I saw. She bought it.

"Wind fever? All that I'm feeling is wind fever?"

"Yep, you, me, Randy, Kelly, and all the animals in this wind are experiencing wind fever, and it's not comfortable, is it?"

"No, no, not at all. Oh dear. I had no idea."

"Well, that's the story of all this wind. It causes wind fever and makes us think unpleasant thoughts and do unthinkable things. For now though, I just need you to get into the canoe so we can get out of here."

"Oh no, I can't paddle! I'm too weak and too tired and too, well, I have wind fever!" She looked back at her feet. Her hands folded in her lap.

I had sold my story too well.

"Okay, I know you're experiencing wind fever, and I get that you're tired and feel weak. But, Jeannie, we have to get out of here before we get stuck again for the night. We need to get to the safety of the canal before the wind picks up again to the point we can't paddle against it. So please get in the canoe."

"No, I can't. I won't."

I went over to Kelly to ask if she minded paddling with Randy. This jewel of a woman said no she didn't mind at all. But what about Jeannie? I told her not to worry about Jeannie. I would get her off the platform and out of the Swamp one way or the other. I just really wanted her to get on the water with Randy so they could reach the canal without too much trouble in the freshening wind.

Kelly and Randy loaded up. Randy hugged his mother hard. She barely had the presence of mind to hug him back.

I helped them shove off. "We'll catch up with you in the canal. Now get going!"

They paddled off with Randy looking over his shoulder every few strokes to check on his mother.

I turned back to Jeannie.

"Okay, Jeannie, you have two options. You can either get in the canoe on your own, or I'll put you in there myself. You know I'm stronger than you, and you know I can do it."

Fall Sky Over Round Top

"Wha, what?"

"You heard me. We have to get out of here, and that means now. You're wasting my time by not getting in the canoe. You don't have to pick up the paddle at all. Just get in the goddamn canoe, Jeannie. Please. Jeannie."

Jeannie sat for another few long anxiety-ridden moments. My patience wore thin.

"Jeannie, I am asking you one last time to get in the canoe on your own. Otherwise I will get you in there myself, and you may not like my method."

Finally, finally, slowly, ever so slowly Jeannie moved. She uncrossed her feet. She moved her hands off her lap to her side on the bench. She braced herself to rise up. Unsteadily she stood to full height, looked at me with those eyes. Those dark eyes that I thought had a bit of blue in them now. Zombie-like she shuffled to the edge of the platform. I helped her sit on the edge to stage herself to get in the canoe. With great effort I kept the canoe from tipping over as she plopped hard into her bow seat. Great. I didn't need her wet too. At least we avoided that near-disaster.

I shoved off from the platform with a good hard push and pointed the bow headfirst into the wind, eastward down the trail, homeward.

As promised, I didn't say a word to Jeannie about picking up her paddle.

I struggled to keep us on the trail in the wind. It blew on to our aft quarter beam in a strong breeze, and I just managed to keep us on the trail most of the time. Occasionally when a big gust hit us, I braced against it to keep from veering off course by sticking my paddle hard into the peat. Those three miles in the Grand Prairie proved to be the most challenging work out I had yet to endure.

It even trumped the infamous "oatmeal paddle" Suzanna I would endure years later when the water levels dipped so low the Refuge allowed only seasoned veterans on the Purple Trail. They knew me as a four decade-plus seasoned veteran. On that paddle it took Suzanna and me an hour to paddle one mile. The water level on the trail through Grand Prairie on that trip was so low it exposed the peat, making it like paddling through thick oatmeal. Now, I paddled by myself in this strong breeze of nearly 25 knots in a fully loaded canoe.

Jeannie sat in my bow. At least she weighed it down so we didn't do wheelies in the now-howling wind.

I remember standing up a few times to pole, but after nearly getting blown out of the canoe, I remained seated. I presented too much resistance to the wind.

In an hour and a half we reached the relative safety of the famous Suwannee Canal. I couldn't have been happier to see that long, straight, monotonous, boring canal. Nearly giddy with joy and relief, I let loose with my signature Swamp holler. I began on low notes at low speed, crescendoing to higher and higher notes and faster and still faster speed and finally ending in a very loud staccato of Ha, Ha, Ha of descending notes.

Yeeeee......Yeeee......Yeee....Yeee...YEE..YEE..HA..HA..HA..Ha....Haa...Haaa...Haaaaa.

Surprised, Jeannie turned around to look at me. The vacant look had been replaced with reigniting awareness.

She turned back around in her seat and reached for her paddle.

She paddled the rest of the nine miles down the canal.

We caught up with Randy and Kelly who waited for us just down the canal from where we turned off out of Grand Prairie. Randy smiled from ear to ear to see his mother paddling. She smiled back at him but did not stop paddling.

Jeannie didn't even want to stop for lunch at Coffee Bay Day Shelter. She asked that we continue paddling. She really wanted to get back home, now. I didn't indulge her request. We were all hungry. I did however take a vote, and no one really wanted me to cook last night's dinner as I said I would. Instead we finished off all the food that didn't need to be cooked. We ate apples and oranges, granola bars, cookies, GORP (good old raisins and peanuts – in our blend it included M&M's), peanut butter and jelly on heels of the leftover bread loaves, cheese on remnants of crackers. Surprisingly we had plenty to eat.

Jeannie barely ate anything. I think I saw her put a handful of GORP in her mouth. Like a horse going home to the barn, Jeannie paddled. She paddled without lifting her head, without changing sides, without uttering a word. With unwavering determination she exceeded my

Emerging Dragonfly

greatest expectations. Considering that I didn't expect her to paddle at all, she really didn't have to do much to improve on that low setting.

Jeannie paddled impressively, even for me, with even, strong strokes. Somehow she had tapped into her inner, heretofore unrealized strength. She had changed.

I don't know when that exactly happened but it had happened, and I had been right there through it all. I didn't know what that change meant. I didn't care. I liked it!

Changelings in nature fascinate me. Jeannie fascinated me. I adored Randy and so very much appreciated Kelly. We were all going to be okay. We were all on the easy downside slope now of a very difficult, physically demanding mountain and for Jeannie an equally, if not even more demanding, emotional mountain.

To Kelly's credit she kept talking natural history with Randy. She pointed out hawks and egrets and vultures and gave him all the information she knew. Randy gratefully absorbed all she gave out.

With Jeannie paddling so intently and skillfully and surprisingly strongly now, we leap-frogged ahead of them by many canoe-lengths. Kelly had to kick it into high gear to try to keep within a respectable range. I kept looking back to make sure they were okay. They were okay.

When we reached the boat basin, Jeannie tried to walk on water to reach the sandy bank. I had to make her wait, wait, wait, okay now, now you can step out on to the bank. She leapt out of the canoe and bolted for her car. She didn't say a word. I have never seen a more determined look on anyone's face than I saw on hers that day. She cranked up her car and spun out of the parking space. Our demure, polite, gracious, smiling beauty queen had metamorphosed into

Suwannee Canal Basin

confident, self-assured, large and in charge. Jeannie ruled her realm, and she didn't even wear a crown anymore. No matter. She ruled!!!

As soon as Randy and Kelly landed, I grabbed their bow and pulled them up onto the bank, so Randy could step out without getting his feet wet. With him out, the bow lifted up, and I pulled Kelly up to the point where she too could get out without wetting her tootsies. Randy hugged Kelly and then wrapped his arms around my waist in a most warm appreciative hug. It really made me feel like a million bucks.

Jeannie skidded her Mercedes into the loading area and began grabbing her and Randy's gear. Randy fell in and did the same. Jeannie did not utter a word.

Kelly and I unloaded the two canoes of our gear and all the camping gear and food coolers. Before I knew it, Jeannie and Randy were speeding out of the parking lot without a word of goodbye or thank you or that stunk or anything. That was certainly a first for me.

Kelly and I looked at each and shrugged and then busied ourselves loading the rest of the gear into the van and then the canoes onto the trailer.

Did I mention how much I appreciated Kelly? What a goddess-send she was.

On the way back to Savannah we stopped somewhere to get a quick bite to eat and continued dissecting each and every aspect of the trip. It was then I learned about Jeannie's situation.

I wished I had known earlier, but there really hadn't been any time for Kelly to tell me, and Jeannie certainly didn't want to clue me in. I guess spilling to Kelly had served as catharsis aplenty.

And spilling to Kelly was easy since they shared a canoe. Working together, paddling to move the canoe down a waterway is an interesting mind-body phenomenon. I have learned a lot about canoe partners that I am sure I would not have learned in normal face to face conversations.

I returned Kelly to her B&B on West Gaston Street that evening. Normally I would have suggested we go out to eat for dinner somewhere nice in Savannah, but really, Kelly and I had shared quite an adventure already. I didn't think anything else would have added to the experience nor the bond. I still clearly remember her after all these many years. I am still grateful she came on this particular trip.

I still clearly remember Randy as he was on his 12th birthday. Today he is a man, most likely an accomplished professional in either law or medicine. Secretly though, I wish he followed his curiosity into science, pure research science. Maybe he did.

You can imagine my shock six months, maybe eight months, after this trip had ended, after Jeannie had whisked Randy away without even a fare-thee-well, when I received a hand-written letter from Jeannie. Addressed to Mother Nature.

Dear Mother Nature,

You didn't know at the time of the Okefenokee Swamp trip for Randy's 12th birthday that I was going through a really rough, brutal, divorce. My husband of nearly two decades with whom I raised two adorable children decided our marriage was over. Only problem was he didn't bother to tell me. Humiliated, embarrassed, devastated, heart-broken, crest-fallen, undermined, etc. are all descriptions that fit me at that time. Not anymore. I didn't think I could endure anything else. I didn't think I could handle one more obstacle. I didn't think I was capable of doing anything beyond what I was already doing. Until that is I went on your trip.

The trip challenged me physically, mentally, emotionally and spiritually. You guided me through it all. I am a better person for it. Thank You!

Just so you know, I was going through a nasty divorce because my husband decided he preferred the company of a much younger woman. He willingly gave up our family to begin a new one with his much younger nurse. I was devastated to say the least. At some point on your trip though, I came into my own. You helped me reach deeply into my own soul, dig down to find my inner self, and pulled out the strength and insights to make my way forward. I changed into the person I needed to be for myself and more importantly the person I needed to be for my children.

Thank You, Mother Nature, for helping me find myself, for helping me draw on my inner strength, the inner strength you knew I had all along and just needed to find again.

When I returned home from that most fateful trip, I set about ensuring my children and I received the support and resources we deserved and to which we were rightfully entitled. I enlisted the help of my dear friend and lawyer Richard. Three weeks ago I married Richard. We joyfully combined our families and have been living happily ever since. His wedding present to me was a big yellow Mohawk canoe with a big white ribbon wrapped around it that I discovered floating in our pool when we returned home from our wedding. I couldn't believe it. It was the best wedding gift a new bride could ever receive!

So, you see, Mother Nature, it is because of you I found my voice. You enabled me to put my feet on the right path. You helped me find again the physical, emotional and spiritual strength I once had long ago that helped me win beauty pageants and then helped me raise two beautiful children. You are my inspiration and my krypton. Thank You, Mother Nature!

And by the way. Richard and I have been happily paddling every weekend since that fateful Okefenokee trip. Our kids love it too and of course especially Randy.

Jeannie was wrong. I didn't help her. She had helped herself. The physical, emotional and spiritual challenge she experienced in the Okefenokee had helped her find her inner strength to get the job done and she had gotten the job done well.

Minnie's Lake Run

CHAPTER 10

Swan Song of the Swamp

Big Water

Spring 2008

Six people were originally scheduled to be on the last trip I ever took with Dr. Bob, the pleasingly plump one. He reserved the dates with me far in advance. I would pack gear and buy and pack food a few days prior to the day it began.

But a week or so out, Dr. Bob called to say that three people had cancelled, leaving only his daughter, son-in-law, and himself. No worries. I really liked small groups. The fewer the better in my book. I had already made up the menu and shopping list. I simply adjusted the quantities down. No problem at all.

A few nights before the trip began though, Dr. Bob called me at home.

"Swamp Goddess, this is Dr. Bob Harris."

"Hey there, Dr. Bob! How's it going? Are you ready to roll?"

"Oh yeah, I'm ready! But, no one else is."

"What? What's going on?"

"Paige and Son-in-Law Bob can't join me now. Something came up, and they just can't come. I'm so very disappointed. I don't want to cancel, but that means it'll be just you and me. I'll certainly understand if you don't want to go with just me, but this truly may be my last trip. I'm not getting any younger. My shoulder hurts everyday now, and I have to take lots of pain-killers just to keep going. I know I can do this one last trip though. Please, Oh Great and Merciful Swamp Goddess, please do this one last trip with me!"

I thought for a minute and said, "Let me think about it and get back to you. I'll call you in a little while."

"Doggone It!" I thought to myself. "He's really laying it on thick, playing the 'this may be the last trip' card. But I've had these dates blocked out for this trip for months now, and that income won't be there if I don't go. I've already bought the food and just need to pack it. On the other hand, I don't really want to go with just Dr. Bob. He'll talk the entire time, and it'll be hard to be nice when I have to listen to him all day long and all night too with no other people to diffuse his prattle. Damn it, what's a Swamp Goddess to do?"

I struggled to make a decision. Finally I concluded I needed the money and really didn't want the extra food wasting away in my refrigerator. It needed to be eaten. I decided to do the trip if he agreed to a few conditions.

"Hey there, Dr. Bob, Cathy, er, Swamp Goddess here. Yes. Yes, I've decided to do the trip with you but only if you agree to a few conditions. Are you game?"

"Well, that's great! But what conditions, Oh Great and Wise Swamp Goddess?"

Minnie's Lake Run

"First off, what's Mrs. Harris' take on this? Is she okay with you and just me?"

"Oh, yes, Mrs. Harris is in complete agreement that I need to go on this trip. As a matter of fact she insists I go. I think I'm getting on her nerves."

No surprise there. From previous conversations I took it that their relationship, while loving and generally full of mutual admiration, wore thin at times, maybe most of the time. I suspected however that she would not know that this trip would consist of just me and him until their daughter Paige spilled the beans while we were actually on the trip.

"Secondly, you know I adore you, but not your running commentaries. So while we're paddling, I'll insist that you be quiet and just observe. We'll see so much more if we, you, simply don't talk. Do you think you can handle that?"

"Well, I don't think that'll be a problem. What else?"

I knew it would be a problem. It was always a problem. He talked about a lot of things: opera, the latest medical innovations and discoveries, social ills, his children, their spouses, his wife, his golf buddies, their spouses, their children, community leaders, politicians of all government levels.

And he sighed audibly, a lot, out of sheer appreciation for the beauty of the Swamp. I appreciated that very much, but it did grate on my nerves at times.

"Your snoring can get to the point of being unbearable. You'll need to either ensure that you won't snore, or, if you do, you won't get angry with me when I wake you up to make you stop."

"Oh, I don't snore."

"Oh, yes, you do!"

"No, I don't."

"Well, Yes, You, Do! Do you remember the night at Round Top when you snored so loudly a bull gator came right up under the platform and bellowed back and shook the entire platform? Oh, wait, of course not. You don't remember that because you slept right through it!"

"Oh, well, okay, that was the one and only time. I'm not a snorer!"

"Okay, then, you're in denial, and I can't go on this trip with you."

"Oh, all right. All right! I'll get a mask or something to keep me from snoring. The very idea! Why haven't you said anything before?"

"I have. On each trip. You seem to have amnesia when it comes to this subject."

We sounded like an old married couple.

"All right, I'm a snorer. There, are you happy now?"

"Good. We're on the right track. Okay, then, to recap,

minimal talking while we're paddling, and very minimal snoring. Good? Good! I think we're all set. I'll meet you at Kingfisher Landing at 9:00 AM day after tomorrow. Good night, Dr. Bob."

"Good Night, My Dearest, Sweetest Swamp Goddess!"

"Nighty Night, Dearest Dr. Bob!" I gagged a bit as I hung up. Sometimes it's hard being deified.

Dr. Bob arrived long before I did and filled the time birdwatching. He admitted he had already spotted a few knot birds, moss birds, and branch birds. Either his eyesight or his binoculars, probably both, needed polishing up. He had a knack for turning inanimate objects into the most interesting new species of birds.

I gave him a warm hello hug, and we exchanged the usual pleasantries. In short order we set about loading our gear for our two-night adventure into my green Mohawk canoe. We would be following the Red Trail. The first night to be spent at Maul Hammock and the second night Big Water.

I really didn't know how this trip would go, but with a leap of faith we launched.

Dr. Bob sat in the stern and politely waited for me to get in. Since he outweighed me by at least two, maybe two and a half, times, I needed to be in the bow. He sighed loudly. The first of many such contented sighs.

Another problem for me with Dr. Bob was that he only paddled on his right side. He tore his left rotator cuff a few years back, and it pained him so much he just couldn't paddle on that side. I wouldn't be able to change sides every mile to balance my muscles out. I anticipated the need for a chiropractor and a deep-tissue massage after this trip.

With the temperature in the mid-70's throughout the day, we paddled without breaking a sweat. Well, at least I didn't. Dr. Bob always perspired. He wrapped a fresh bandana around his forehead each day to keep the sweat out of his eyes. He wore sunglasses but never a hat. On this day his turquoise bandana handsomely set off his already darkening tan. I never saw him apply sunscreen. Not once.

By MM 3 (mile marker three) we were in orchid alley. The rose pogonias (also called snakemouth orchids by someone who overreacted) were splendidly elegant with their dainty frilly lower-lip petals and even daintier slender green leaves. In striking contrast the electric purple floppy petals of the statuesque blue flag iris towered over them. Hooded and trumpet pitcher plants just budding out stood still, erect and tall. Their flower heads drooped over like a supplicating errant husband in an apologetic hangdog posture. The never wets, or golden clubs, were mostly in flower as well. The bright canary yellow of their tips contrasted with the lovely ivory white and pink rose of the lower bands along their rods. Later in the season, when the tiny flowers on the clubs swelled into delicious sugar-infused seeds, I would be snacking on them for quick energy.

Rose Pogonia Orchids (*Pogonia ophioglossoides*)

I only had to remind Dr. Bob twice that we were in silent paddling mode. The first time, when he began to sing, I turned my head to give him the evil eye, and effectively nipped his aria in the bud. The second time I initiated the conversation when I asked about a new medical technique he had introduced on a previous trip. He waxed eloquently about it but then just kept on going. I said enough for now. He complied.

Around MM 7, on a narrow stretch of trail lined with elegant fragrant white water lilies, we saw an amazing display of tried and true wildlife survival strategy.

We came upon a mother Wood Duck leading her clutch of ten or so fluffy downy ducklings down the waterway ahead of us. When she noticed us approaching, she sharply clucked to her brood. They responded by "evaporating" into the adjacent hurrah bush. I use the term "evaporate" because Dr. Bob and I earnestly searched for those ash-colored ducklings in the shrubbery, and we just couldn't see them anywhere. They disappeared like little Caspers into the greenery.

In the meantime Momma Wood Duck gave the most convincing broken-wing performance I have ever seen. She feigned trying to fly but just couldn't quite get up off the water with that broken wing. She had to rest with so much effort taking so much energy out of her. She was so convincing I almost thought she did have a broken wing, and I knew better!

When we came within a few canoe lengths, she tried again to get away in spite of her broken wing. She repeated her impressive performance several more times until all of a sudden her wing miraculously healed. Divine intervention, no doubt.

Of course we were just far enough away from her precious babies that we didn't pose a threat anymore in her mind anyway. She did her job admirably and convincingly.

To this day that encounter remains the best display of broken-wing behavior I have ever observed.

Of course, Dr. Bob and I had to discuss this, so I gave him a waiver on conversation. Mother Wood Duck deserved an Oscar for her Best Performance in a Leading Role. Leading humans away from her precious flotilla of ducklings.

We paddled on for the rest of the day, enjoying our great good fortune of pleasant temperatures and light breezes. The breezes kept us comfortable without impeding our progress, quite a rare treat in the Okefenokee.

We reached Maul Hammock around 4:00 PM, and I really needed to stretch. Paddling continuously on my left side made that entire side of my body knot up. Even my hips felt as if putty had been packed into the joints. Dr. Bob didn't seem any worse for the wear. He unfolded slowly, bobbled a bit as he balanced in the canoe. Then with great effort he lunged out of the canoe, plopping onto the platform, then scooching up a bit to get away from the edge. The fat rippled up and down his body as he moved. He looked a lot like a bull elephant seal scooching his great girth up the beach at Año Nuevo.

"AAAAHHHHHH! OOOOOHHHHHH! SSSSSIIIIGGGHHHH!"

He sighed a sigh of great relief and gratitude to be on a relatively solid surface where he could lay supine. He sprawled out as if to begin making a snow angel.

I let him stay there for a bit too long, and in no time he sawed logs. I admired him for that. Falling asleep anywhere, any time is really enviable. I do it too. Just at the wrong times in the wrong places, like at dinner parties with important dignitaries.

I unloaded the canoe and set up the kitchen and pitched my tent and then his. I checked the chemical toilet and cleaned the seat and door handles and left the door ajar to air it out a bit more than the wind turbine had managed thus far. I knew Dr. Bob would pull out his incense in the morning when the toilet would get its highest use. He referred to it as "the Tardis" à la Dr. Who. Didn't matter. It stunk just the same by any name.

I deliberately struck a pot louder than necessary with a large metal spoon. The noise had the desired effect. Dr. Bob jumped, snorted, and sat up.

"Well, what a fine, fine day. Fine as frog's hair, Swamp Goddess. A fine day indeed. What's for supper?"

"Yes, a good day, a fine day. We're having your favorite meal of course, zucchini in marinara sauce."

He tried to twist around to glare at me, but couldn't quite do that, so he shifted his upper torso quickly and shook the entire platform. I tried not to laugh. I still visualized him as a bull elephant seal, and the image got to me. I laughed anyway.

"Oh you mock me, Swamp Goddess! My heart breaks. And why in the world do you keep serving me zucchini when you know I hate that godawful stuff and those goddamn Red Delicious apples that have absolutely no taste whatsoever?"

"Oh relax, I'm just yanking your chain. We're not having zucchini and no Red Delicious apples are violating the sanctity of the food box."

He grunted and twisted back around. His feet dangled off the platform. I brought him a cup of merlot. I knew what would come next.

After sipping his wine for a few minutes, sure enough, right on cue, he began.

O sole, 'o sole mio, sta 'nfronte a te,

sta 'nfronte a te!

Ma n'atu sole cchiu` bello, oje ne',

'o sole mio, sta 'nfronte a te!

O sole, 'o sole mio, sta 'nfronte a te,

sta 'nfronte a te!

O sole, 'o sole mio, sta 'nfronte a te,

sta 'nfronte a te!

He actually had a lovely baritone voice that he now raised to the top of the trees. Impressive.

I applauded and sat down beside him to sip my first cup of merlot.

"We had an excellent day. You were quiet when I asked you to be, and you paddled well, even though just on the one side. No way around that, huh?"

"Nope, no can do."

We chatted on until I heard the water boiling over, causing the stove to sputter. I jumped up to rescue the flame from being doused and to finish dinner.

Dr. Bob relished the marinara infused with real lean ground beef and chopped fresh onions, sliced organic canned mushrooms, freshly chopped celery, and a bit of fresh basil and dried parsley over semolina noodles. A small salad balanced out the carbs and protein. We topped off dinner with Pepperidge Farms Chocolate Collection cookies. I loved those tasty darlings, and the only time I allowed myself the indulgence was after paddling a really long day. Between the two of us we ate half the box.

After supper we had a few more cups of wine before the sun set and before the mosquitoes descended on us. I puffed on my Portofino Macanudo for as long as

Billy's Lake with Cypress in Fall Colors of Russet

its billows of sweet smoke kept the tiny blood-sucking invaders at bay. When their sheer masses overcame my smoke screen, I retreated to the safety of my tent.

Dr. Bob on the other hand, sat a while longer, appearing not to mind the onslaught. In fact he seemed to be relishing it in a sad sort of way. It seemed as if he savored each tiny annoying, stinging assault on his body. It must have made him feel alive. With each mosquito that sucked his blood, he left a bit of himself in them and therefore in his beloved Okefenokee Swamp. Corpuscle by corpuscle.

The Okefenokee Swamp was his absolute favorite place on this good Earth. What better place to leave a part of yourself?

He nodded in agreement as he conversed with himself in his head. Eventually he let me in on the conversation.

"Yo there, Swamp Goddess, asleep yet?"

"Nope, just reading a bit."

"Okay, good. I told my children, all of them, I want my ashes sprinkled along Minnie's Lake Run. I want them to play Beethoven's Fifth while they sprinkle me around. They don't have to say any prayers or chant any incantations or such. Just sprinkle me with that symphony playing."

"I'm making note of this."

"Ha, very funny. No, really. I'm serious. If something happens to me while I'm, while we're out here on this trip or the next or the next, you have to promise me my wishes will be carried out. Capisce?"

"Si, Signore, I promise. I'll carry out your wishes." I went back to reading.

I knew the mosquitoes should have carried him away by now. But perhaps all that blubber insulated him against them. Naw, I saw him flinching and enjoying it!

As soon as the sun set, the chorus of frogs – crickets, carpenters, southern leopards, pigs, rivers, greens – cranked up. As night descended upon us, the chorus grew deafeningly loud. I relished it. This is why I loved the Red Trail. This phenomenon alone was well worth the entire trip. For most, it is so loud they just cannot sleep through it. I can sleep through almost anything, but I didn't want to sleep through this glorious chorus of aggrandized, amplified, amazing amphibian amorousness.

One of my friends described this as time-traveling back to the Jurassic. When I listen to that delightfully, incredibly loud chorus all night long, I day-dream of dragonflies with three-foot wingspans and long necked brontosauruses roaming the prairies and swimming the lakes. What an incredible time that must have been! I also thank Mr. Spielberg for bringing those fascinating creatures to life for us on the big silver screen.

In no time at all my Science News magazine hit my face, and I jerked awake. My headlamp still burned, so I slid the switch to off. I could hear Dr. Bob softly snuffling in his tent. At least it wasn't the full-on roar that typically issued from his tent. I chuckled when I noticed his tent walls actually heaving in and out, flexing with each of his heavy breathes. What a character!

The next morning dawned beautifully with a low fog ghosting right over the water. The Swamp mist wrapped around us like a dream sequence on a movie set.

Every surface – tents, platform, canoe, gear box, cooler, duffle bags, shoes, everything – dripped in the heavy dew. I changed out of my sleeping clothes into my outfit du jour. I selected a rose flowered bikini, contrasting quick-dry light gray pants, matching rose-pink quick-dry long sleeved shirt, coordinating rose flowered bandana, and my gray and pink water shoes. All set, I emerged from my tent to fire up the stove for Dr. Bob's coffee and my tea.

Over my many years of guiding trips, among all the routine tasks, the chore I found most tiresome was making coffee, especially cleaning up the damn coffee grounds. Early on in my camping career I used instant coffee, and in my book that worked very well. But remember, I never drank coffee. Still don't. To the hardcore coffee drinkers, instant coffee does not work. It is an abomination. So I switched to perking coffee in a stovetop percolator. Eventually I decided that my coffee drinkers could at least learn to drink cowboy coffee to eliminate the need for an extra piece of gear, the percolator.

I brew cowboy coffee the way a hard core coffee drinker taught me years ago – in a regular pot with the grounds thrown in loosely. The grounds naturally settle to the bottom after the pot is removed from the heat. To really make cowboy coffee correctly however, you employ centrifugal force to concentrate the grounds even more firmly into the pot bottom. To do this you take the pot in one hand and with outstretched arm you rotate the pot rapidly in a windmill motion so your arm looks like a propeller attached to the side of your shoulder. Since Dr. Bob could not perform this maneuver anymore, I did it. Not happily, but I did it, for him.

I realized how seriously coffee drinkers need a strong dose in the morning on a trip with my friend Kim and her young daughter Ava Grace. Ava, at six years old, became an intrepid camper and paddler after she tired of her mother going off on trips with me and leaving her behind in the care of her father. Ava Grace insisted on accompanying us the next time a trip to the Everglades came up. Taking a six year old on an extended wilderness camping trip is risky.

To young Ava Grace's credit, the trip went incredibly well. Ava Grace sat in the bow seat of her mother's double kayak for the five-hour paddle out to Camp Lulu Key. She reported that it really only seemed like one hour. Good kid.

On our first morning on Camp Lulu Key while still in our tents, I heard Ava Grace excitedly chatting away to her mother about all the really cool things Aunt Cathy said we would see in the tide pools. "And Momma, the tide is out. I can see those tide pools, and we need to get our clothes on and get out there. We just have a lot of things to see! Momma? Momma?"

Kim's barely audible, un-caffeinated slow drawl responded, "Baby. [long pause] Baby. [even longer pause] Momma needs you to stop talking now. I haven't had my first cup of coffee, and I just can't do this just yet. Please be quiet, Baby."

I lit the stove to make the much needed morning coffee. Kim's mug with "Okay, But Coffee First" on it, already had been placed by the stove the night before.

Morning Coffee Making

With my brewing done, Kim's day could dawn.

And so I made Dr. Bob's morning coffee. He appreciated it so much he kissed my hand as I delivered it to him. For several minutes I heard him savoring each long sip. He gurgled as he sucked up a partial mouthful through the tunnel of his narrowed lips. Next he cleared his throat, gargled with a half mouthful and then let loose with.......

Tutti mi chiedono, tutti mi vogliono,

Qua la parruca, presto la barba, presto il biglietto, Ehi!

Figaro... Figaro... Figaro... Figaro... Figaro...

Figaro... Figaro... Figaro... Figaro... Figaro!!!

Man, he sounded great even this early in the morning and on only one cup of coffee! He let the last "ro" of the last "Figaro" roll on for many beats longer than the composer intended. His voice echoed across the still damp morning air. Not even the insects had cranked up yet on this new day.

I applauded loudly, "Bravo! Bravo! Bravo!" But I held off adding, "Encore".

After a hearty breakfast of bacon, eggs, toast, and lots more coffee for him and tea for me, we broke our small two-person camp and loaded everything back into our waiting canoe. Today we would paddle 11 miles to Big Water. The trail would take us through prairie for the first three or so miles and then through a series of small lakes, really just wider parts of the trail, and then through what are referred to as the batteries.

The batteries are thickets of small trees and large shrubs through which the trail has been cut. There is no place to get out to stretch your legs since it is so

Entering a Narrow Trail Through a Battery

thick it is literally impenetrable by the human body. In about a third of the batteries the trees and shrubs overhang the trail, so if you are paddling a kayak, your double-bladed paddle hangs up in the vines and branches.

The batteries make some people claustrophobic. I really like the batteries. They are very intimate. To me it feels like I am getting a big Swamp hug every time I go through them.

I stretched out both sides of my body in preparation for the forced paddle solely on my left side to Dr. Bob's right-side-only paddling mode. I apologized to my muscles and promised a nice professional massage when I returned home. I entered our comments in the platform log – "Fabulous froggy albeit loud love chorus all night long".

And then just like that, we were off!

The most memorable part of this day's paddle came at about the third mile at MM 15. I had already reminded my loquacious paddling partner of his promise to be quiet, and he piped down for a little while. I think his morning aria had him all jacked up.

Even before we left the platform, we could hear the incredibly lovely trumpeting of a resident pair of Florida Sandhill Cranes not too far away. The male trumpeted at a lower pitch and slower frequency to the female's higher pitch and faster vibrato. They called together in a beautiful, hauntingly endearing duet.

Florida Sandhill Cranes are slightly smaller and lighter gray than their cousins, the overwintering Greater Sandhill Cranes. The Greater Sandhills arrive when the first cold weather sends them fleeing their northern feeding and nesting grounds. They arrive in impressive numbers usually by mid-November in the Okefenokee and further south into Paynes Prairie in central Florida. They begin flying back north as soon as they feel the weather will stay warm enough to provide food.

Unless the two different species are near each other, the only way I can tell them apart is by the numbers in their groups. Florida Sandhill groups consist of a mated pair and typically, from spring on into fall, a chick or two. The Greater Sandhill groups typically number from five to as many as 20 or more adults.

For the Florida Sandhill Cranes courtship takes place in winter during which the pair trumpet musically while bowing, leaping, jumping and touching necks. They spread their wings to their full span of six and a half feet in quite a lovely display of avian mutual adoration and admiration.

Sandhill Cranes mate for life. Over the years of their union, pairs learn to rely on each other to successfully raise their one or two chicks to adulthood. One to three eggs are laid on a large loose aggregation of grass, sedge, and reed. The mats can be as large as 40 inches across and up to five inches thick. Both parents incubate the eggs with typically only one chick surviving chickhood. Within eight hours of hatching, a chick will follow its parents. It will stay with them for about eight months until the parents are ready to procreate again.

Sandhill Cranes are omnivores. In the Okefenokee the Florida Sandhills dine on frogs, snakes, small fish, seeds, roots, and insects. At Round Top platform in particular, Florida Sandhill Cranes are so used to campers, they forage nearby in spite of loud talking and raucous laughter and general camp racket. I guess when the getting is good why let a bit of human noise interfere?

On this day though, as we rounded a curve in the trail, I literally came eyeball to beak with a parent Florida Sandhill Crane and chick. I mean just feet

Year-Round Resident Sandhill Crane

away. I froze. To his credit Dr. Bob did too. For a few all too brief minutes we became part of this parent and chick's experience. I couldn't believe it! Thrilled, I drank in every part of each bird.

The parent, hard to say if mom or dad, but I'll go with mom, towered over my head since I was sitting. The slate gray feathers covering her back were huge. Her gold eyes looked deeply into mine as if to ascertain friend or foe. The bare red patch of skin on top of her head seemed so much redder than I expected. Of course I had never seen it this close up before. From a distance it looks washed out. She craned her neck to look at Dr. Bob and then craned it back to look at me. She sized us up and apparently decided we were not a threat but rather, perhaps, really weird-looking friendly creatures.

Our canoe, still coasting forward, slowly ran up onto a peat blowup adjacent to her nest. The surprisingly calm mother didn't bolt nor cluck to her chick to bolt. They both lingered for a few more seconds thoroughly inspecting us.

The yellow downy chick came up to the top of mom's legs. It had a face only a mother could love, so ugly while at the same time incredibly cute and adorable. The downy feathers on its head stuck out every-which-a-way like the unruly mane of Einstein's disheveled gray long locks of his later years.

Mom looked me in the eye one more time. She appeared cross-eyed looking down her long pointed beak that could have easily taken out one of my eyes with a quick thrust of her head on her gracefully curved neck. The curve in the long necks of herons, egrets, and cranes provide thrusting power for striking at prey or defending against predators.

Cranes however mostly use their feet to fend off would-be predators by kicking. Apparently and fortunately we did not seem a threat. In a few more seconds mom slowly turned, clucked a short soft cluck to her chick. They both slowly, quietly, deliberately walked away from us, the interlopers, into the tall broom sedge.

Wow! Wow! Wow! I wanted to leap for joy and shout out our great good fortune! What an incredible experience! What a very rare interaction indeed! To my credit though, I held my exuberance in check. I didn't want to give mom any reason to doubt her positive assessment of us.

Having such rare interactions with wild animals only happens when you are out in wild places. And only when you are respectful enough of the wild environ and its inhabitants to become as much a part of it as you possibly can. By being quiet and by paddling quietly we had accomplished this for a few precious minutes. What a fantastic reward!

I could have ended the trip right then and there and been completely satisfied. I just didn't think it could get any better than that. But we were miles away from Big Water platform, and we needed to push on.

Somewhere around MM 19, an hour or so after we stopped for lunch, Dr. Bob began struggling to paddle. His right arm ached, and he said it felt numb. Of course we both wrote it off to his rotator cuff issue. So we stopped every 15 minutes after that to rest and so he could shrug his shoulders. I took the opportunity to stand up and stretch my muscles and apologize, again, to them.

By the time we reached the gorgeous cypress stands of Big Water on our final two miles to the platform, we were both glad for the current that now carried us along. Dr. Bob stopped paddling all together except when he needed to maneuver the stern around a log. I kept the bow pointed down the gorgeous waterway, moving a bit faster than the current. Without him paddling I could at least change sides periodically.

Around 5:30 PM we reached Big Water platform. We were much later than our typical arrival time of 4:00 PM, but at least we made it before dark. I helped Dr. Bob out of the canoe and told him to rest while I unpacked and set up his tent and then mine. I popped the cork off a bottle of pinot noir and handed him his first cup. He took it but sat it down beside him instead of lapping it up.

Swamp Goddess Enjoying a Pensive Moment (Photo by Suzanna Black)

When I began to prepare dinner, he asked if we could just have hors d'oeuvres instead of a full meal. Even though starving, I decided to do as he wished. I somehow thought perhaps he just wanted to hear the natural evening sounds of the Swamp and not the typical loud noises of the kitchen and the stove. I complied.

A most pleasant evening ensued. I sipped my first cup of wine rather quickly. Perhaps because my muscles on my left side were screaming and I, in dire need of relaxing, had another cup. And then another to accompany the cheese and crackers and Fuji apple slices. I opened up a bag of mixed nuts and threw a handful of those into my mouth. Dr. Bob ate sparingly. He sipped his first cup of wine rather than going at it with his typical enthusiastic gusto.

He seemed introspective. I didn't really pay close attention. I just wanted to dream about momma Sandhill and her fluffy Einstein-coifed chick in the warmth of my sleeping bag.

The three cups of wine brought on relaxation quickly. Morpheus' arms stretched out to welcome me.

I tidied up the kitchen and asked Dr. Bob if he wanted anything else. He said no, he was satisfied. I repackaged the leftovers and secured them in the cooler and food box safe from any marauding raccoons and mice. I tied the lids securely with line and shoved them under the picnic table bench for extra insurance. While leaning down to sit the opened bottle of pinot next to Dr. Bob, I kissed him goodnight on his bald head. Uncharacteristically he didn't ask me to stay up to chat. He seemed content to sit by himself with his feet dangling over the side of the platform. He patted the hand I placed on his shoulder as I kissed his head. He smiled sweetly, serenely, contentedly, gratefully.

Several hours later I awoke to answer the call of nature

and, while answering, I viewed the night sky as I typically did. You have never really seen the night sky until you are in a wild place away from the lights of the city. The night sky in the Okefenokee is spectacular. With no moon to dim the stars you get Carl Sagan's "billions and billions". Unbelievable, really. I picked out the Big Dipper and the Little Dipper and Orion and Delphinus and Taurus and the Pleiades and Cassiopeia. What a lovely display!

Once, on a houseboat trip into the heart of the Everglades, I heard soft sobbing coming from the stern. Since most of my guests were in the salon, I couldn't figure out who my unhappy guest was. I went aft to find our dentist from St. Augustine with his head in his hands. Not knowing his background, I did what any compassionate person does and put my arm around his shoulder. He accepted my comforting gesture and eventually his sobs subsided. He told me he had never seen the night sky before. I didn't know what he was talking about. Surely he had looked up and seen the night sky before now. "No. I haven't. I've lived my entire life in or near a city with bright lights that obscure the night sky. I didn't know there were so many stars. This is unbelievable!" He teared up again. I told him I bet that this would not be the last time he would see the night sky in a wild place far from the stab of city lights. He solemnly promised.

Then I noticed Dr. Bob. He lay on the edge of the platform on his side with his legs precariously sticking out over the water. Had he moved a bit too much one way or the other, I would have surely heard a loud splash and a lot of colorful expletives. Funny though, I didn't hear him snoring. I got out of my tent and went to him. He wasn't breathing. He was stone cold.

OH MY DEAR GOD!!!!

Red Trail Lined with Lily Pads

I pulled his stiff legs back onto the platform, and his torso nearly went off the other end. My adrenaline kicked in, and I managed to heave his entire bulk back from the edge before I had a disaster on my hands. Well, I guess I already did! I turned him onto his back to check his vital signs. No heart beat and no breathing. Rigor mortis had already set in. His bent legs stayed up in the air. I began CPR anyway.

One and two and three and four and five and breathe. One and two and three and four and five and breathe.

I pumped with both hands on his chest and, as taught in CPR at that time, gave him a breath. I got into a rhythm, but I knew I couldn't keep up this pace for long. There was no one else around to spell me. I would need to conserve my energy to get us out of the Swamp. I gave up. I patted his big chest and told him how sorry I was.

Then I realized this is exactly how he wanted to go. The big galoot had planned this all along. He knew this trip would be his Swamp Swan Song!

For the rest of the night I sat beside Dr. Bob as he lay motionless on the platform. His cup of wine nearly full. The bottle drained half down from my three cups and his one. I finished off the bottle and toasted him repeatedly.

The only dead person I had experienced up until that time had been my grandfather Oscar Lavira Hamilton. He was really my step-grandfather, but, since my real grandfather Jerry Robert Pearsall West died long before I was ever even a twinkle in my parents' eyes, Oscar was my beloved Grandpa. My grandfather Oscar died in his bib overalls as he sat in his tractor seat while plowing the corn stalks under to prepare the field for his next crop of soybeans.

As is the custom at old-timey country funerals, I was told I needed to kiss my grandfather goodbye as he lay in his casket. At 13 years of age this was not going to happen. I wanted to remember my Grandpa Oscar as I had seen him that morning, in his bib overalls with some of breakfast's bacon grease still glistening on his stubbly chin. I did not want to kiss the man in the casket who sort of looked like my grandfather but who wore a black suit, which someone bought and put on him. He would have never worn one of those willingly.

I sat next to Dr. Bob's cold and still body. I too was

cold and still. I didn't really know how to handle this. But when in doubt, I sing.

Ave Maria, gratia plena. Maria, gratia plena, Maria, gratia plena, Ave, ave dominus, Dominus tecum. Benedicta tu in mulieribus, Et benedictus, Et benedictus fructus ventris, Ventris tui, Jesus. Ave Maria.

I sang in Latin and then in English and then several times through in Latin again. Just a year prior to this trip, I recorded "Ave Maria" in a friend's recording studio as well as "Amazing Grace" when I received word my friend in the Everglades, the Sociable Hermit Mike Ward, had died.

The last time I had seen Mike alive, he made me promise that I would sing at his funeral, and he specifically requested "Ave Maria" and "Amazing Grace". Since he requested cremation, I knew his funeral and memorial service would be when his children and most of his friends would be on the island. That would likely be between Christmas and New Year's. I knew I most likely would not be able to go then, so to fulfill my promise I recorded those two songs. I sent one CD to his son and another to our mutual friend Brenda. Brenda reported that I sang beautifully during the ceremony and no one had a dry eye on the beach that day. I doubt my voice moved those present to tears, but rather the lyrics and haunting melodies and the memories of Mike touched his mourners.

I moved on to "Amazing Grace".

Amazing Grace, how sweet the sound, That saved a wretch like me. I once was lost but now am found, Was blind, but now I see. T'was Grace that taught my heart to fear.

*And Grace, my fears relieved. How precious did that Grace
appear The hour I first believed. Through many dangers,
toils and snares I have already come; 'Tis Grace that
brought me safe thus far and Grace will lead me home.
When we've been there ten thousand years Bright shining
as the sun. We've no less days to sing God's praise Than
when we've first begun. Amazing Grace, how sweet the
sound, That saved a wretch like me. I once was lost but
now am found, Was blind, but now I see.*

I sang as many hymns as I could remember from my
days of attending my parents' Southern Baptist Church.
I surprised myself, I remembered parts of "Rock of
Ages", "Up from the Grave He Arose", "Angels We Have
Heard on High", "The Old Rugged Cross", "How Great
Thou Art", "The Benediction".

Some of the lyrics I didn't like, but their melodies stuck
with me all these many decades. They somehow seemed
appropriate now even though I knew Dr. Bob did not
attend church and certainly would have never set foot
inside a Southern Baptist Church. I could have sung
rock-and-roll songs, but that didn't seem appropriate.

Okefenokee Sunrise

As the sky began to lighten up just before dawn, I did sing one song that I adored. I first heard Cat Stevens, now Yusuf Islam, perform it, and to my great delight it actually had a place in the Southern Baptist Hymnal, "Morning Has Broken".

Morning has broken, like the first morning, Blackbird has spoken, like the first bird. Praise for the singing, praise for the morning, Praise for them springing fresh from the word. Sweet the rain's new fall, sunlit from heaven, Like the first dew fall on the first grass. Praise for the sweetness of the wet garden, Sprung in completeness where His feet pass. Mine is the sunlight, mine is the morning, Born of the one light Eden saw play. Praise with elation, praise every morning, God's re-creation of the new day.

When the first rays of sunlight pinked the eastern sky, I rummaged through the food box for the tea bags and breakfast. I would need a lot of energy for this day. I would be paddling in the stern. I would be taking my friend down his favorite place in the entire world, down Minnie's Lake Run, and I needed to do it right.

For a few moments in between songs I thought about making a funeral pyre out of the platform or giving him a Viking funeral by setting fire to the canoe. Neither of those options would have worked. I had a dead body on my hands, and I needed to deliver him to the proper authorities and to his family. I just needed to get him back to dry land. It was going to be hard enough just getting him into the canoe.

I packed up our tents and all the food into the cooler and gear into the gear box and set them near the edge of the platform off to one side. They were strategically placed for loading into the canoe. I cinched the canoe close to the platform in as many ways as I had line to stabilize it. My first priority would be to get Dr. Bob into the canoe, and that was going to be a gargantuan task.

Fortunately when rigor mortis set in, he was already in a sitting position, so at least I had that going for me. I knew I had to get this right the first time. If I didn't, I would be towing Dr. Bob like a harpooned whale behind the canoe, and that, besides being undignified, would be extremely hard to do. I thought long and hard on how to get him into the canoe without flipping it and without overshooting him into the water.

I unzipped his sleeping bag and laid it out flat beside him. I rolled him over onto it to get him completely inside it and then zipped it up. I reasoned that he would be easier to control if I slid him into the canoe on slippery material. The nylon exterior of his sleeping bag seemed like it might do the trick.

To my great surprise and relief, he slid rather easily to the edge of the platform. Good thing I lifted weights in between those paddling trips. I laid him over on one side and then nudged him a little bit, then a little bit more. He teetered and then upended right into the middle of the canoe. His great weight sent the canoe slamming down deeply into the water with only a scant inch of freeboard. The stern lifted up and dipped the bow under the water briefly, and then the reverse happened. I watched with my mouth wide open in an "Oh My God That Really Worked" expression!

I bailed the little bit of water out and then thought about trying to prop Dr. Bob up into a sitting position in the middle of the canoe. I decided that would require way too much effort. In the process I just might tip the canoe over, and then I would really be in a pickle. I shifted him around in the bag so his feet and lower legs that landed up on the thwart joined his head, torso, and thighs on the canoe bottom. Not elegant nor graceful, but it worked.

Next I loaded the rest of the gear into the bow and the spaces around him and behind and under my seat. I needed to keep the bulk of the weight in the rear to have better steerage. I checked around the platform for loose ends.

My routine is to write the required trail log entry just before shoving off. I simply entered "What a Night! Thank You Dr. Bob for All the Many Good Memories." I wondered what those who came to the platform on

Reflections in Minnie's Lake Run

following nights would read into my log entry.

I shoved off. The canoe's weight seemed easy to handle. Perhaps my burden lightened by the promise I made to Dr. Bob. I would get him to his family and make sure they sprinkled him down Minnie's Lake Run while Beethoven's Fifth played in the background.

I paddled in easy, long strokes and changed sides periodically. The strong current at Big Water already pushed us along towards Stephen Foster State Park just fine.

I don't exactly recall what I saw along the way that day. In retrospect, I remember the wildlife seemed still. Birds sang but sat in branches as if paying their respects. I nodded to them in appreciation. Even the knot birds, moss birds and branch birds bent and swayed their homage. I paddled on rhythmically and didn't even stop at the day shelter at Minnie's Lake for lunch nor to answer the call of nature.

Surprisingly I didn't get hungry nor did my bladder fill up. I just kept paddling at a slow steady pace. I needed to complete my mission. Actually I didn't really want to engage in conversation with anyone I would likely meet. I didn't want to explain the big bundle in the middle of my canoe. Dr. Bob, even swaddled in his large blue sleeping bag, still looked odd and pretty much like a corpse.

Just past Minnie's Lake, the Run begins. It narrows, causing the previously slow-moving current to race through and around the buttressed trunks of the many cypresses lining the Run. Operators of motor boats find it hard to control their craft and unfortunately crash into the trunks. All of the tree trunks sport deep gashes where boat bows repeatedly hit and chip out new chunks. Each inexperienced helmsperson adds an assault, deepening and widening the gashes.

In a canoe an experienced paddler noses the bow into a turn letting the current swing the stern through the turn. I had no problem weaving us in and out of the turns down Minnie's Lake Run. Halfway through, I remembered that Dr. Bob wanted Beethoven's Fifth playing as he traveled down its sinuous passageway. I hummed it as best as I could remember.

DA da da dahhh, DA da da dahhh, da da da dahhh, da da da dahhh......

A few canoeists and kayakers paddling against the current met us, and we exchanged pleasantries. They wanted to know where I had camped and couldn't believe I had soloed. I didn't tell them I had the company of my precious cargo.

My surreal journey down the Run reminded me of the ancient rituals of the pharaohs for some reason. I thought how cryptic of me not to share Dr. Bob's last journey in his earthly form with anyone else. I focused on getting him back to Stephen Foster and went over in my mind what I would say.

I would seek out longtime Park employee Marilyn Finger Yeager whom I have known for decades and tell her and the Park superintendent at the same time. That way Marilyn could vouch as to the fine upstanding person I am and not something else others may think when you show up with a corpse on your hands. Especially when the corpse is not your own husband, but another wife's husband, a wife noticeably not present.

As I made the last few turns in Minnie's Lake Run, I felt the wind pick up. I heard it whistling through the upper branches. The tree tops bent as stronger wind rushed in behind the first salvo. In the distance I could see the sky darkening. Not good. When I reached Billy's Lake, the wind blew straight into my face. Oh

South End of Billy's Lake

great, just what I needed. I leaned into it to keep a low profile. I put my full shoulder into each labored stroke.

In no time flat the wind increased into a full breeze with white caps exploding everywhere. Really bad. I struggled to keep us moving forward. Dr. Bob seemed heavier now. In this heat-sucking wind I broke a sweat. I had not done that before. I worked hard to just move the canoe one length ahead. I felt nauseous. I felt stuck in oatmeal. I could barely move.

The wind picked up even more. In the distance I saw the low black roll clouds of the volatile leading edge of a fierce storm. Really, this was my reward? Bolts of lightning streaked down from the black roll towards the water. The tallest tree tops exploded into fireworks. Furious Thor unleashed his full arsenal.

I called upon my sister deities for strength. I called upon the flora and fauna of the Swamp for energy. The wind sapped my drive. I faded fast.

It now blew a gale. I had no recourse but to seek the safety of the side of the lake and hold on for dear life. I tied off the bow to a cypress knee and held the stern in place with my hand on another. The wind blew in a mighty and nearly deafening roar. My hair blew every which way and stung my eyes. I couldn't keep them open. My situation became dire.

The wind lathered the surface into three- to four-feet standing waves. The canoe rocked violently up and down and pitched to and fro. It took on water faster than I could bail it out. We began sinking in the dark roiling water.

Dr. Bob floated up off the canoe floor. I reached for his bag, but he slipped over the gunnel and then beneath the surface. I lost him. Oh My God! I screamed. But the wind sucked up my scream. I screamed again, but nothing seemed to come out this time. No one heard me. I screamed again. And again and again and again....

~~*~*~*~*~*~*~*~*~*~*~*~*~*~*~*~*~

"Hey, Swamp Goddess, Swamp Goddess! Wake up! Wake up! You're yelling loudly enough to wake the dead!" Dr. Bob shook me.

I looked up into Dr. Bob's very-much-alive, tanned round face. I blinked a few times just to make sure I wasn't still dreaming.

"You're alive! You're alive! You're really alive!"

I grabbed his face and pulled it to mine, kissing him squarely on the lips.

He sat back on his haunches, very surprised and very pleased, "Oh My Dear Swamp Goddess, I don't know what you were dreaming, but I like it!"

He looked down for just a minute and then back at me, "Er, and just for the record, we won't be telling Mrs. Harris about that kiss, now, will we?"

~ ~ ~ ~ ~

Epilog:

This was the last Swamp trip I would ever have the privilege of sharing with Dr. Bob. It was a most memorable trip indeed.

For a few months afterwards, I received e-mail messages from him, revealing decreasing nimbleness in his fingers and failing cognition. Words were misspelled and his sentences fragmented.

Grass Pink Orchids (*Calopogon pulchellus*)

The first pronouncement was cancer of the kidneys. A few weeks later the inevitable diagnosis came. He had aggressive brain tumors, glioblastoma multiforme.

Within a few months Dr. Bob was gone.

His children knew what to do. They had been on Okefenokee trips with him.

I was not invited to spread his ashes with the family, at the request of his wife.

No matter. I had already given him a fine send off, if only in my dreams. We had shared the trip that turned out to be Dr. Bob's Swan Song of the Swamp.

I imagined that in some of his dreamy murmurs in his last days, he said something on and off about "a fuzzy little Einstein and handing out an Oscar to a duck."

I am sure he must have also smiled happily as he cooed about "his sweet kiss from the Swamp Goddess".

November 1996 - FR-Dale Williams, Hound of Baskervilles, Dr. Bob Harris, Mary Wall, Suzanna Black - BR-UIP, SG, UID (Photo by Dr. Bob Noble)

(This photo, taken from a print saved by Suzanna who sent it to me in February 2019 after discovering it in her files, is a blast from the way past. My co-leader Dale Williams, in the lower left corner, and I ran this trip for Wilderness Southeast in November 1996. Suzanna, still a paying customer at that time, is in the lower right corner. We are at Trader's Hill Recreation Area in between the city limits of Folkston and the entrance to the Okefenokee Swamp at Suwannee Canal Recreation Area. We look clean, fresh, and rested because this is before we entered the Swamp on a long paddle on the Red Trail. As we set up camp that afternoon, a hound befriended Mary Walls who named him Hound of the Baskervilles. Dr. Bob Harris, a family practitioner turned radiologist, thought that none of us were ever inoculated enough with healthy bacteria, so he gladly "loved" on the hound. In stark contrast, fastidious pathologist Dr. Bob Noble did not touch the nasty dog. He agreed to snap the photo on Mary's camera because he did not want to be near nor seen with the very smelly hound. Mary, a horse caretaker, did not mind his odor one little bit. As I recall Dr. Bob Noble did not hug any of us either and especially not Mary after the trip as is customary. Dr. Bob Harris, of course, did.)

Afterward

Thank you for joining me on my great adventures! It has been a true pleasure to share the Great Okefenokee Swamp with you. I have been privileged to paddle with so many like-minded people over these past many decades and with the hope of continued good health, sound mind and lasting physical strength, I will be doing so for another many decades. Hope does, after all, spring eternal!

The images accompanying my stories were taken in the last decade on my cell phone, which is so much more convenient than taking along extra gear such as a real camera and the necessary batteries. I am truly impressed with the quality of the images cell phone cameras take and so I use mine. I have only had a cell phone since the 1990's, so the images in this book are relatively recent. I have tons of slides taken on various cameras and paddlers have sent me hard copy photos, but those have long since succumbed to the ravages of living in a high humidity climate. I do have my memories though and can see my companions clearly as if these adventures happened just last week. Through my words I have tried to capture their spirits and personalities for you. I hope I succeeded.

But, using my cell phone as my camera as convenient as it is, does have a downside. It uses up precious battery life. One of the first things I tell those entering the Swamp for the first time, is to put their cell phones on airplane mode. Cell phones endlessly and fruitlessly search for satellites the entire time thereby draining batteries quickly and even more so in cold temperatures.

Cell phone service in the Swamp is very spotty and dependent on weather conditions. Sometimes I can call from most anywhere, but on a subsequent trip, I am lucky to get even one call out. I can always text though. Still cell phones are wonderful and provide a marginal sense of security. No matter what your service provider is, you will always be able to make one call out, so it is best to save it for that one emergency call you might need to make. After that it depends on cloud cover and where you are in relationship to your service provider's nearest tower.

The very first trip on which I ever carried a cell phone spanned seven days into the back country of the Everglades. The phone, actually a bag phone, dates the trip to around 1983 or 1984. On that particular trip we were far into the heart of the Everglades when one of my guests, George, presented symptoms of a heart attack. An evacuation by kayak would have been about 15 hours straight of paddling. So, I fished out the new-fangled bag phone from the nose of my kayak, turned it on and jumped for joy when it's little power light went from blinking red to steady green. Instinctively I dialed 911. An emergency operator answered. Whew! She immediately deployed a helicopter and within a

Paddling Buddies - Bryan "Water Bear" Schroeder, Scott Taylor, Kris Williams Carroll, Swamp Goddess, Todd "Swampman Muss" Mussman on Minnie's Lake Platform

half hour it passed right over us. Even though I provided the exact coordinates, I still had to fire off an orange smoker flare so they could pinpoint our exact location. George had indeed suffered a heart attack but survived the ordeal and went on to live a good life for many more years thanks to that bag phone and his emergency crew and medical care-workers!

Anyway, when you paddle with me, you may end up in one of my stories. I'm just giving you fair warning!

The images in this Afterword are of those brave souls who have ventured with me into my beloved Okefenokee Swamp but have yet to end up in one of my stories. They are all aware though they just may be included in a story before long. They have all consented to let me post their images and state their names.

A few sneak previews of the many other stories yet to be written and may include those paddlers you see in the images that follow.

Matters of the Heart: One of my dear paddling buddies, Bryan, convinced me to accept his friend Todd on one of my annual fall friends' trips. Bryan asked and so of course I said sure. That first day we paddled 12 hard miles into a headwind on the Red Trail to Maul Hammock. This particularly tough paddle tested everyone's endurance. Over dinner and wine as we chatted about the beauty and concomitant hardships of the day, Bryan let it slip that Todd had just had open-heart surgery three weeks prior to this trip. I nearly fell off the platform! I just couldn't believe that, a.) Bryan didn't share this important tidbit of health information previously, as in before the trip, and that b.) Todd paddled like a champ!

Birthday Surprise: On one fee-based trip into Swamp decades ago, a guest, Jerry, signed his application and pledged that the information he provided was correct. He registered his age as 74 along with his birthdate and I noted he would celebrate his 75th on Big Water Platform, so I added a cake and candles to the food supplies. On the night we camped on Big Water Platform, I pulled the cake out and lit the candles after dinner, not 75 though, just some representation of it, otherwise we would have lit the wooden platform on fire!

As we all sang Happy Birthday, Jerry beamed. Someone remarked how fit he looked for 75. The Birthday Boy just couldn't contain himself any longer and very proudly blurted out that in fact he just turned 90!

Lions and Tigers and Woodpeckers, Oh My?: On another trip, a guest, Gary, ducked every time a woodpecker came near and cringed when he heard one. His companion Darlene, would chuckle with him at some inside joke. It wasn't until the second day into our trip as we unloaded our canoes for the night, Gary's canoe started to pull away from the platform with him still in it, so he instinctively

Swamp Goddess and Friends (George Reeves, Frank Wooldridge, SG, Todd Recicar, Marsha Henson, Calvin Zippler)

stuck out his only free limb and I grabbed a hold. You can imagine my horror when I pulled off the lower portion of his prosthetic "wooden" leg! Oh yes, that really happened.

There are many more stories that will come to light in a future book, but for now, Dear Reader, thank you for spending time with me and my fellow and sister paddlers. We had a great time and I hope you did too! I encourage you though to get out and paddle in the one and only Okefenokee Swamp on your own, with friends and/or family. Actually, just paddle anywhere. Hike anywhere. Just get outside. It is well worth your effort and you never know what adventures you will have if you don't. I do know this, the benefits of doing so will be more rewarding, much more rewarding, than not doing so!

Thank You for Reading!

Cathy J. Sakas

Swamp Goddess

July 2020

Swamp Selfie

Abbigail (Abby) Rigdon Murphy – Swamp Goddess Cover Artist

Tom Cofer, George Reeves, Calvin Zippler, Cathy Sakas, Suzanna Black

Jody Patterson, Annabel Patterson, Cathy Sakas, Suzanna Black, George Reeves

George and Suzanna

Jody and Annabel Patterson

Robin Young Roberts

Sandy Prucha (Doctor Sister Sandy)

313

Calvin Zippler

George Reeves

Dr. Sr. Sandy Prucha and Michelle Riley

Theresa Wexler

Chip Campbell

Scott Taylor and Bryan "Water Bear" Schroeder

George Reeves Tempting Fate

Swamp First-Timers Geoff Bulpitt and Ben Peek

Kris Williams Carroll, Scott Taylor, Bryan "Water Bear" Schroeder

Jody Patterson

318

Scott Taylor on Green Trail

Theresa Wexler at Round Top Platform

Acknowledgements

As is the case with anyone achieving a success, I didn't arrive at producing this book all by myself. There are many people and resources I must acknowledge.

As mammals we are not born with an instinctual brain to help us survive in our environment. Humans are helpless at birth through the early years and beyond. We have reasoning brains that must be taught. We must be nurtured along the way until we can manage on our own; albeit, some of us never fully achieve that level.

I am definitely the product of an amalgamation of input.

The culmination of my knowledge about the Great Okefenokee Swamp comes from experiencing it first hand and then using resources to understand completely what I saw, heard, smelled, touched and even tasted. Yes, an experiential professional interpretive naturalist is what I am and I use all of my senses to explore and experience my surroundings.

Much of what I learned initially comes from spending time with other naturalists in the Great Okefenokee and then mostly from what I learned on my own by using field guides and binoculars and pocket microscopes. Today the use of apps on cell phones are invaluable instant resources for identifying and learning about a flower or an insect or a bird, almost anything you encounter.

However, my first and greatest teacher is and will always be John "Crawfish" Crawford. He took me on my first trip in the Okefenokee as his bride back in 1976. We remain colleagues and more importantly friends. He is a fount of knowledge.

Dick and Joyce Murlless, partners with Crawfish in Wilderness Southeast (WiSE), and all the many wonderful staff naturalists/guides over the many decades, taught me so much about interpreting and interacting with guests on our WiSE trips.

I thank all my friends who have braved hot days, cold nights, torrential downpours, swarming mosquitoes, strong headwinds and still enjoyed the beauty of the Swamp with me. I learn from them in so many ways. Some are in photos in the Afterword.

I thank Ben Goggins for lightly but expertly editing my stories and more importantly for helping me find my writing rhythm and style.

I thank Jody Patterson for painstakingly formatting the text and images and for adding her flairs exactly where they needed to be.

Abigail (Abby) Rigdon Murphy created the ultimate vision of Swamp Goddess and her drawings grace the front and back covers.

My huge thanks really must begin with my outstanding parents. My mother, Katherine (Kay) L. West Sakas, took older brother Jeff and me to beaches along the southeastern coast and for two years in New England any time she could, and that was, thankfully, quite often. Those early years of beach outings catalyzed an emerging naturalist into a life-long nature professional and advocate. At age six, my father, Joseph (Joe) Sakas encouraged my ever-evolving interest in science by buying my first microscope. Two years later I received my first telescope and a few years after that my first chemistry set and dissection kit. I continued to receive great scientific tools and gear from him for the rest of his life. My mother, while encouraging my science orientation, really would have preferred a daughter who liked to wear frilly dresses and flowers in her hair. Instead she abided small dead animals, insects and plants dug out of my pants pockets collected on my way home for later dissections and investigations. All received proper burials in our backyard with tiny Popsicle stick crosses. Each cross bore a thoughtfully unique name.

My thanks goes to my brother Jeffrey (Jeff) L. Sakas as well. Even though we share the most genes of anyone on this good Earth, we couldn't be more opposite in most things. I am three and a half years younger and unlike him have always been more comfortable outside in nature. Some of my earliest recollections of outside time together are baiting his hook with wiggly worms when fishing with our grandmother. I made a leaf collection for his seventh grade science project and then later created his bug collection for a high school project. To this day, when together, he will call me to dispatch a palmetto bug or spider. Spiders I lovingly transport to the outside while palmetto bugs typically don't make it that far.

My seventh grade science teacher gets a shout out as well. Mrs. York made us research and write about something we were most afraid of in nature. I wrote about spiders and as a result I adore spiders to this very day. That was her point. If you are afraid of something, you most likely just don't understand it. Smart teacher!

In college I had so many great professors who mentored me in biology, chemistry, physics, astronomy, meteorology, physiology, etc. I soaked up everything like a sponge and they were quite happy to "feed me" whatever they had and when I had used them up, they gladly directed me to other resources. I received my Bachelors of Science in Biology from Armstrong State University in 1976 and followed that up with a Masters of Education in Science several years later from the same institution. Armstrong is now Georgia Southern University, Armstrong Campus.

I would not have made it through Inorganic Chemistry and Physics had it not been for the special tutoring I received after class from a handsome, tall, skinny redhead. I knew Christopher (Chris) R. Morris understood the terminology and math of those complicated courses and he patiently helped me pass those hard early classes with ease. Twenty five years later he proposed and I accepted. To this day he still helps me understand quantum electrodynamics, quarks, radio bursts, Higgs bosons and other physical science topics my natural science brain doesn't as easily grasp.

I gratefully acknowledge all the many professional field guides I have used over the decades. Most are Roger Tory Peterson's, but then there are the field guides produced by David Allen Sibley, National Geographic, Paul Humann, National Oceanic and Atmospheric Administration (NOAA), etc. There are just a whole slew of field guides in my personal library and I am grateful for each author's time and expertise for creating these essential resources.

I am also very grateful for the instantaneous convenience of the apps PictureThis and iNaturalist. These are wonderful resources for identifying and finding out about whatever it is in nature you want as long as your cell phone has enough battery life.

The Worldwide Web is just chock full of resources making the world of nature literally your oyster and for that I am very grateful. I love oysters.

It would be impossible to attribute each fact stated in these stories to one specific source, which is why I again say that the professional interpretive naturalist I am today is because it took a world of nature and a vast community of naturalists and research scientists who published their data, and I eagerly read, to create me and for them I am and will always be eternally grateful.

Cathy J. Sakas, aka Swamp Goddess
Naturalist & Okefenokee Guide
July 2020

Postscript (November 2020):

Holy Cow! It's déjà vu all over again.

As I write, the mining company Twin Pines Minerals, LLC, is threatening our beloved Okefenokee Swamp. The Alabama-based company has again petitioned the Army Corps of Engineers for a permit to mine Trail Ridge, the Swamp's eastern natural boundary. Trail Ridge is an ancient shoreline with abundant sand repositories, rich in titanium dioxide.

The company presents the endeavor as harmless enough. That's predictable. But it is not harmless, not at all. Issues abound with potential impacts that are not reversable.

First, the very hydrology of the Swamp would be disrupted. The open mining process proposed to extract the titanium ore would penetrate to damaging depths. The Swamp's watery lifeblood would be irrevocably damaged.

Second, the operation would bring constant noise and light pollution. The naturally dark night sky would be no more. The roar of throbbing machinery would be the new soundtrack. Everyone who has ventured into the great Okefenokee cherishes the dark sky illuminated only by starlight. The rising moon over the Swamp is an ethereal experience. The Okefenokee has always offered a healing escape from a noisy world, filled with only natural sounds day and night.

The wilderness experience that has always drawn visitors to the Okefenokee would be ruined. The many jobs and businesses associated with this ecotourism in nearby Folkston and Fargo would suffer greatly.

The Okefenokee is a great wilderness. As with any great wilderness, it is up to those who value it to be forever vigilant, to be its advocates, to be its champions. That's where I stand.

This is now the third time our great national treasure in Georgia's backyard is at risk. This is the third time I am speaking up. Please join me and the thousands of others as we raise our voices. Let's keep our wilderness safe. By way of vigilance and advocacy, we must be the Lorax.

About the Author

Paddling with The Georgia Conservancy in the Okefenokee (Photo by Andre Turner)

Cathy J. Sakas
Educator/Producer/Naturalist/Author/Guide

Cathy's lifelong love of our ocean began on Virginia's southern Chesapeake Bay. Since 1976, armed with a B.S. in Biology and M.Ed. in Science (Georgia Southern University - Armstrong Campus, Savannah, GA) Cathy served as a naturalist/guide for Wilderness Southeast. She also produces, writes, hosts and narrates television documentaries and her works include two Emmy Award winning nature series for GPB-TV called *Coastal Naturalist* and *Secret Seashores*, a special on the human and natural history of Georgia's barrier islands. She also hosted and served as consulting naturalist for a multiple Telly Award winning nature series for Turner South entitled *The Natural South*.

Most recently she co-produced *Shifting Baselines* with partner Mehmet Caglayan that aired on GPB-TV in November 2019. Concomitantly for 15 years beginning in October 1998, Cathy worked with NOAA Gray's Reef National Marine Sanctuary serving as ocean science educator, scientific diver and certified pilot of the submersible DeepWorker 2000 as well as an Aquanaut. Since officially retiring from NOAA in 2014, Cathy serves locally on behalf of our great global ocean through stewardship and advocacy with several ocean related organizations including Ocean Exchange and Gray's Reef National Marine Sanctuary Foundation and Tybee Island Marine Science Foundation. She also helped establish Maudlin Pond Press, LLC.

Cathy serves as naturalist for SCAD's Sustainable Design Department's Biomimicry Class and in her spare time is lead singer for a local band called The World Famous Crabettes. She lives with husband Chris Morris in the Treehouse he built in the woods of southern Effingham County, GA with wild animals and a few cats that have adopted them.

Most recently they have been enjoying viewing NEOWISE Comet from the Star Deck Chris thoughtfully included in the Treehouse's design.

CPSIA information can be obtained
at www.ICGtesting.com
Printed in the USA
LVHW010156281122
734107LV00003B/69